◄ FRONT COVER

1 • Chilled Corn-Turtle Bean Salsa

2 • Authentic Salsa Cruda

3 • Oil-Free Avacado Salsa

4 • Citrus Salsa

INSIDE FRONT COVER ►

1 • Peppered Pear-Raspberry Salsa

2 • Banana-Coconut Salsa

3 • Cherimoya-Lychee Salsa

4 • Blackened Tomato-Mint Salsa

5 • Krazy for Kumquats Salsa

SALSA

P.J. BIROSIK

MACMILLAN • USA

Macmillan General Reference
A Simon & Schuster Macmillan Company
1633 Broadway
New York, NY 10019

Library of Congress Cataloging-in-Publication Data
Birosik, Patti Jean
Salsa/ P.J. Birosik. — 1st Collier Books ed.
p.   cm.
Includes index.
ISBN 0-02-041641-5
1. Salsas (Cookery)   2. Cookery, Mexican.
3. Cookery, American—Southwestern style.   I. Title.
TX819.S29B57   1993   92-35699   CIP
641.5972—dc20

Cover Design by Susan Newman
Cover Photographs by David Bishop
Book Design by Anne Scatto
Illustrations by Lauren Scheuer

10 9 8 7 6
Printed in the United States of America

Happy are those who dream dreams

and have the courage to make them come true

CONTENTS

ACKNOWLEDGMENTS

Thanks and appreciation to my editor, Justin Schwartz; to Madeleine Morel, my agent, for her years of untiring effort on my behalf; and to the friendly people of the Southwest and Mexico who cheerfully answered my incessant questions about the inspired cuisine and beautiful lands that we share. A special thanks to the pueblo tribes and other indigenous Americans who opened up to this sincere, searching *gringa*; I've taken your teachings to heart.

INTRODUCTION

A well-prepared salsa is a fiesta for the senses. Colorful, brightly flavored, sharp and sweet, hot and spicy, yet oh so "cool," these zesty side dishes can be used to complement any meal from appetizer to dessert. No wonder salsa is outselling ketchup and becoming America's king of condiments.

In this book four distinct styles of salsa are presented: uncooked, cooked, cocktail, and a combination of cooked and uncooked ingredients. They were inspired by over twenty years of travel throughout the Southwest and Mexico, and refined in my own kitchen for maximum flavor and appearance impact. Each recipe carries at least one serving suggestion, but remember: There are no rules! Feel free to experiment by adjusting ingredients to taste and pairing salsas with your own favorite meals.

Uncooked, or raw, salsas are deceptively simple in appearance and yet must balance opposing textures, flavors, and spices in an attractive and tasty manner. They are only as flavorful as their ingredients, so it is important to utilize only the highest quality fruits and vegetables at the peak of their individual seasons. Recipes range from brassy and bold, to sweet and inviting; uncooked salsas are never shy or retiring, and so are best served with simply prepared meat, poultry, or steamed vegetables, or tossed with cold pasta. Of course, most chip dip salsas are also raw. An assortment of

sharp knives, a potato peeler, and a citrus zester are important tools in making uncooked salsas.

Cooked salsas are not as fussy as Continental sauces but possess a similarly smooth, velvety consistency and underlying richness. Dairy products are rarely used, so these salsas are slimming alternatives to heavy béchamel and hollandaise sauces. Most cooked salsas require a larger amount or a greater variety of herbs and spices than raw salsas; it is important to learn how to adjust a cooked salsa recipe to taste since fruit and vegetable flavors can vary from one preparation to the next. A blender or food processor is essential in successfully preparing a cooked salsa.

Some salsa recipes combine both raw and cooked ingredients, usually with the raw, texture-enhancing items being added to the cooked sauce. Temperature is of great importance here, so pay close attention to serving directions; a limp, lukewarm salsa can be disastrous.

A new category that I've only recently begun to explore is the salsa cocktail. Good enough to drink, these robustly flavored, nonalcoholic salsas are blended into juice; you have the option of enjoying them as is or adding tequila or pepper vodka as desired. For maximum flavor impact, make your own tomato juice base according to the recipe given, then prepare the cocktail. More fun than a Bloody Maria! If you have a centrifugal juicer, use it; if not, a blender works fine for these spicy libations.

This book contains a glossary of items that are commonly found in authentic Southwestern larders and lists of exotic ingredients featured in the recipes. Under each heading is vital ingredient information and useful tips to make your salsa preparation extremely easy. If you cannot locate a particular item in your local supermarket or specialty store, an appendix lists over a dozen mail-order sources; write to inquire about their catalog and product lines, enclosing a self-addressed stamped envelope for the reply.

Many people who savor spicy meals have most likely discovered the nasal nuisance that I've dubbed the "salsa sniffle," a mild but annoying runny nose triggered by ingesting fiery foods. *Gustatory rhinitis* is not an allergy but a reaction to the stimulation of certain chemical receptors in one's mouth. A reflex response is launched, ending with profuse nasal drip. What to do? Keep the handkerchief handy until scientists at the National Institutes of Health in Bethesda, Maryland, come up with an effective therapy; they're working on it.

One can lessen the effect by decreasing the amount of heat in the salsa. Easy measures include seeding and deribbing all chile peppers used and eliminating such ingredients as caribe, chili powder, and crushed red pepper flakes. Substituting less spicy chile peppers is another trick; try using a jalapeño instead of a serrano or a serrano instead of a habanero, or substitute a mild green chile pepper for any of the above. While this tempering tip may lessen your salsa sniffles, it will also lessen the flavor of the dish; you may just wish to savor the salsa as given in the recipe and use lots of tissues! While the ingredients used in this book range from beets to pomegranates, an authentic salsa should possess an element from at least three of the following categories: sweet, sour/tart, spicy/hot, savory, herbal, aromatic. Without this

3 of these ingredients

tripodular balance, the recipe usually fails to titillate the taste buds and entice the senses. Finding this artful marriage of ingredients on your own can take months, even years, as many Southwestern cooks will confirm. So use this book as a starting-off point, a push in the right direction, and an inspiration to achieve your own personal salsa savvy! I wish you luck, and let me know how you're coming along.

SALSA INGREDIENTS & TECHNIQUES

The simplest salsas include one or more types of tomato, onion, and chile pepper. These common kitchen staples can be combined in hundreds of ways, causing the finished product to turn out pungent, powerful, mild, sweet, or incendiary. The art is knowing how to marry different varieties of these basic ingredients in order to create a tasty salsa. Once this is mastered, you can take advantage of flavored vinegars, herbed oils, and exotic spices to customize a simple recipe and create a unique taste sensation.

In this chapter you will find descriptions of many basic salsa ingredients and exotic items included in these recipes that you may not be familiar with, plus numerous tips that will make preparing both cooked and uncooked salsa a joy.

Achiote

Rich orange- to brick-red–colored achiote, or *Annatto*, seeds, used after being ground into a fine powder, add a lovely golden color and earthy flavor to food. Should be used in conjunction with other spices or chile peppers for maximum effect.

Avocados

The bumpy-skinned Haas, which turns from green to black when ripe, possesses a rich, buttery flesh and sweetish flavor. Slick, green-skinned Fuerte avocados stay green when ripe and have a more watery consistency and soapy taste. Haas are preferred for these recipes, especially when bought green and allowed to ripen on a sunny windowsill.

Berries

Gooseberries, elderberries, pyracantha berries, hackberries, and manzanita berries all grow wild in the Southwest, but none are suitable for fruit salsa. Stick with more

common strawberries, raspberries, blackberries, and boysenberries for the recipes in this book. You may have to cut larger berries in half in order to keep them in proportion with other ingredients. When you can find them, wild mulberries make a wonderful contribution to salsa, though wild juniper and bearberries should be reserved for jelly making or dried for seasoning.

Cacti

One of the rewards for desert living has been access to the delicious pads, flowers, buds, and fruits of wild cactus plants. Mescalero Apaches living in the Sonoran Desert that stretches from central Arizona to Baja California and into Mexico, have found over one hundred uses for the *agave*, also known as the maguey or century plant, including a method of distilling mescal, the basis for tequila. While tequila is featured in this book, more than a dozen varieties of cacti have edible parts; for convenience, we'll stay with one plant that is now being offered fresh in the specialty produce section of supermarkets as well as bottled in the Mexican food or gourmet department: prickly pear cactus. Also known as flat opuntia, this plant features distinctive stems growing out of one another and long sharp spines on both pads and fruits. The pads, or *nopales*, are flat, measuring 6 to 8 inches in length in a round or oval shape. If possible, purchase the young, new, green pads called *nopalitos* rather than the more mature, yellowish-green nopales. Spines should be removed very carefully using tweezers; residual spines can be scooped out using the tip of a small knife or the end of a potato peeler. Some people burn off the spines, but I find this lends an acrid taste to the young pads. Nopalitos do not need to be peeled, but mature pads should be peeled before use. Prickly pear fruit, also known as *tunas*, are small oblong globes about 2 inches in length that turn reddish purple when ripe. After the spines are removed and the globes are peeled, the deliciously sweet fruit can be diced or mashed and used in salsa.

Chayote

This pear-shaped squash, also known as a *mirliton*, is making its debut in supermarkets as a 4-inch-long, light green, hard, slightly bumpy vegetable. Chayotes also range in size from 3 to 8 inches, and can be creamy ivory or medium to dark green. While some cooks prefer peeling off the skin, I feel that this is like peeling a zucchini. The seed, however, must be removed prior to using raw or cooking. Its uncooked flavor is similar to cucumber; cooked, it tastes like summer squash.

Cherimoya

This apple-shaped fruit has a thick, plated skin that is inedible and must be removed prior to use. After seeding, the soft white flesh can be diced or crushed into pulp. It tastes like a strawberry-flavored banana with a hint of pineapple. Handle the flesh delicately when chopping, using the sharpest of small knives for a perfect cut.

Chile Peppers

The word *chile* has been traced back to the Aztec Indians of central Mexico and describes many types of hot peppers used in preparing uncooked and cooked salsas. Varieties in this book include the following:

ANAHEIM: mild, 2-inches wide at the shoulders and tapering, 6-to 8-inches long, usually glossy green but partly or entirely orange-red when vine-ripened. These peppers are also known as New Mexican green chiles but are actually grown in California and are milder than the New Mexican variety. They are sold fresh from spring through autumn, or canned preroasted and skinned, whole or diced, under the generic name "mild green chiles." Anaheims add flavor without much heat. Dried

anaheims are available all year round as whole red pepper ristras, ground into powders, or in preparations such as bottled pastes and sauces.

ANCHO: see *Poblano*.

ARBOL: very hot, 2-to 3-inches long, usually sold when mature and red but can be mottled green and red or solid green. This skinny pepper is used to add heat, not flavor.

CARIBE: the dried, crushed version of New Mexico red chiles, also known as pizza pepper flakes. This is not a powder.

CAYENNE: very hot, bright red, 1/2 inch at the shoulders and about 4 to 6 inches long. When dried, pods and seeds are ground to make a spicy hot pepper of the same name. Lots of heat, virtually no flavor.

CHILI POWDER: A medium-hot commercial preparation that mixes some or all of the following into a brick-red powder: cayenne, paprika, cumin, salt, cloves, coriander, black pepper, turmeric, and crushed chiles.

CHIPOTLE: see *Jalapeño*.

DRIED CRUSHED RED CHILE FLAKES: a commercial preparation usually made from dried red New Mexican or Anaheim chiles. Pieces are individual, rather than ground, with flecks of red, yellow, brown, and even black among the flakes. Pizza parlor pepper flakes are a common example of this type of preparation. Flakes add both heat and flavor, ranging from medium hot to very hot depending on what peppers are used.

HABANERO: dangerously hot, 2-to 3-inches long and around, green to golden orange when ripe. These puffy and bloated-looking peppers are one hundred times hotter than the spicy jalapeños, to date the hottest pepper on earth. Adds much flavor as well as firepower.

HATCH: a variety of the New Mexico green from Hatch, New Mexico, the chile-pepper capital of the world. Can be freely substituted with New Mexico greens.

HUNGARIAN WAX: medium hot, 3-inches long, mild yellow. Let ripen to canary yellow at room temperature before cooking or buy peppers with orange spots. Adds flavor with some heat. Also marketed under the generic name of *guero*.

JALAPEÑO: medium hot to very hot, 2-to 3-inches long, deep green to green with red splotches; can be vine-ripened to deep red. This most popular pepper varies in heat depending on the season and where they were grown; a good rule of thumb is to taste a small piece and adjust the recipe accordingly. Adds more heat than flavor, depending on the spiciness of the individual chile. Dried jalapeños are called *chipotle;* they are medium hot to very hot and brown, with roughly textured skin. These smoked, slightly charred jalapeño peppers add a rich texture and complex flavor to salsas. Chiles are usually found canned or bottled rather than sold individually; the reddish brown sauce should be included with the peppers themselves in any recipe use. Adds both flavor and heat.

MULATO: see *Poblano.*

NEW MEXICO GREEN: mild to hot, 1 1/2-inches wide at the shoulders, tapers, 4-to 6-inches long, medium green, and glossy. As sweet as the Anaheim but spicier, this is the basic chile pepper for not only salsa but virtually all Mexican and Southwestern cuisine. When ripened late in the season, these chiles turn bright to brick red and are called New Mexico red peppers; they are often dried in bunches.

PASILLA: hot and smoky, 1-inch wide at the shoulders, 5 inches in length, purplish black with wrinkled skin. Also called *negro* when dried. Often confused with poblano.

PIMIENTO OR PIMENTO: a plump red pepper about 2-inches wide at the shoulders and almost 4-inches long. Fleshy, very sweet, and sometimes spicy, it is

usually cut into strips and pickled along with green olives, although it can be found bottled by itself. When dried and ground, it is called *paprika*.

PIQUIN OR PEQUIN: tiny, 1/4 inch in diameter, pellet shaped, orange red to dark reddish brown, and extremely hot. Chiles can be used whole as a flavoring but should be removed prior to serving. Usually used crushed or ground into powder. Substitutes include similarly shaped and incendiary peppers: *japones, serrano seco,* and *arbol.*

POBLANO: mild to medium hot, 2-to 3-inches wide at the shoulders, tapering, 3-to 5-inches long, and dark green. A type of poblano is marketed in California under the name *pasilla*. A true poblano is puffier than a pasilla, is shaped like a bell pepper with collapsed sides, and possesses a sharp tip, while the pasilla has a blunted tip. Adds flavor with some heat and is usually hotter than an anaheim and milder than a New Mexican green chile or jalapeño.

Poblanos are called *ancho* or *mulato* when dried, although anchos are usually deep red in color while mulatos are dark brown to almost black. The chile's skin is dry and extremely wrinkled. Both dried forms possess an intense smoky flavor that complements their medium-hot heat. Chiles are sold whole or ground into a brick-red powder.

SERRANO: very hot, 1 1/2-to 2-inches long, fairly thin, light to dark green. Often confused with the jalapeño; look for shine since jalapeños have more sheen. Adds both heat and flavor. Canned peppers are available but are usually pickled and so must be rinsed well before use.

HANDLING CHILES

The flesh of a chile pepper is flavorful but not spicy; the seeds and ribs contain the heat, so remove them for milder salsa. If possible, handle fresh chile peppers using

rubber gloves; touching your mouth or eyes with bare fingers during or after the handling of chiles can be painful. If you do develop a burning sensation, immediately flush the affected area with cool water. The spicy aroma of numerous peppers can cause watery eyes or a runny nose, so work in a well-ventilated space, opening windows or switching on a fan to disperse the heavy aromatic scent.

ROASTING CHILES

Place one or more chiles, as needed, on a grilling rack and broil approximately 4 inches away from heat until the top side is toasty brown (or blackened, as specified in the recipe); turn the pepper over and repeat the process. The skin will blister and split; remove the roasted skin entirely (or partially, as directed) before preparing salsa by peeling with fingers (use rubber gloves) under cool water. Some people prefer to place roasted chile peppers inside a sealed plastic bag or in a plastic-covered heat-resistant bowl and let them "sweat" for fifteen to twenty minutues prior to removing skins by hand. You can also roast chiles by spearing them on a metal skewer and exposing them to an open flame (gas range, campfire, miniature propane blowtorch) until the skins darken, then peel as described above.

Cilantro

Also known as Chinese parsley or fresh coriander, this spindly-stemmed plant boasts delicately fringed green leaves that have a lemon-soapy taste. Quite addictive to most but repulsive to some, the flavor adds an extra dimension to uncooked salsas and cooked pestos. In most cases the stems are discarded, with the leaves being utilized whole or minced. Unfortunately, there is no shortcut to picking off the leaves individually; discard the yellow or brown leaves. Sold in bunches, each cilantro bunch

will yield between 3/4 to 1 cup of leaves. Cilantro will last three to five days in the crisper portion of the refrigerator before wilting. Dried coriander flakes and coriander powder are available in the spice section of supermarkets; each adds some flavor, but not as much as the fresh herb and should not be freely substituted.

Epazote

This is a pungent herb with pointed, serrated leaves on a spindly stem; also known as Mexican tea weed. While rarely available fresh—except in tropical parts of Mexico—it is available dried as flakes and ground into powder in Latin specialty and gourmet food stores. Many Mexican cooks use this herb in bean pots, believing it eliminates flatulence. I recommend it in some cooked salsa recipes. The taste is unusual and may need to be acquired, so use sparingly and to taste.

Onions and Lilies

Yellow, red, white, and green onions are all integral parts of salsa when used alone or in combination. To vary the flavor of a cooked or uncooked salsa, substitute one variety of onion for another, increasing or decreasing the amount used as desired. Varieties include the following:

BERMUDA ONION: medium to large, round with flattened sides, ivory, sweet, available April through June.

CHIVES: extremely thin, long, green stalks, delicate oniony flavor. Substitute for green onions to make salsa less pungent.

GLOBE ONION: common yellow onion, globular, in various sizes, available all year round.

GREEN ONION OR SCALLION: very slim white ends plus long, narrow, hollow green stalks, pungent, available all year round. Use the white and green parts in recipes unless instructed otherwise.

PEARL ONION: small, white, oval, sweet, available all year round.

PURPLE ONION: large, globular, deep red to almost purple, mild, very sweet with pungent overtones, available all year round.

RED ITALIAN ONION: large, globular, red, extremely mild, very sweet, available March through September.

SCALLION: see Green Onion.

SHALLOT: red, lavender, and pale green varieties; lavender is sweeter, never spicy, and adds an elegantly subtle nut flavor to salsa.

SPANISH ONION: large, globular, golden brown, mild, sweet, available from September through March.

PEELING PROBLEMS

Most salsas feature one or more onions. Peeling them can be difficult and time-consuming. Try boiling globular onions for two to three minutes; extremely large onions may take one to two minutes more. Drain the boiled onions, then plunge them into a bowl of ice water. This will not only make the skins peel off more easily but will also make the onions less pungent.

QUICK CUTS

While chopping green onions is often easy to do with a sharp knife, I find that using scissors on the green stalks is not only faster but gives more control. Mincing chives with scissors is almost a necessity since pressing down on the tender shoots to secure an even slice on a cutting board bruises them, releasing their vital flavorful juices.

ONION ODOR

Like chile peppers, onions give off a very strong scent that can induce tearing or sniffing. Make sure the workspace is properly ventilated, opening windows to increase air flow if necessary. If the aroma is still overpowering, try a trick I picked up from watching a photographer loading film in the Arizona sunshine: Peel and prepare the onion inside a large bag! While shutterbugs must use black opaque bags, I use a clear plastic bag (from the dry cleaner). Spread the bag on the counter and open the bottom edge facing you. Slide the cutting board, knife, and onion inside, letting the bag's top surface drape over your forearms and hands. Prepare the onion as usual, and notice how most of the fumes stay inside the bag!

Soap and water are often not powerful enough to remove onion odor. Try wetting your hands with cool water, pouring salt into one palm, and washing your hands with the salt as you would normally. Rinse with plenty of cool water. Always finish by applying hand lotion.

Passion Fruit

Known as *purple granadilla* in Mexico and parts of the Southwest, this fragrant egg-shaped fruit is usually 2-to 3-inches long with a wrinkled deep-purple skin when ripe. The yellowish-green sweet pulp is filled with tiny edible seeds. Do not try to remove the seeds when making salsa, but do remove and discard the skin.

Persimmon

Persimmons must be fully ripe (very soft, deep orange) and in season in order to be used in salsa; firm yellowish-orange fruits will need to be ripened. Place unripe persimmons in a paper bag with a red apple and seal the bag; let it stay on a counter or shelf for one to three days, or until ripe. Store the ripe fruit in the refrigerator.

Pine Nuts

Wild pine nuts, also known as *piñons*, have been gathered by aboriginal tribes for over a thousand years. These are the tiny, thickly-shelled, almost square-shaped brown nuts that pine cones release during season; the heavy shell must be removed prior to use. For these salsa recipes you will be using only shelled pine nuts, about 1/4-inch long or smaller, cream- to tan-colored, and slightly plump at one end. Shelling piñons takes hours, but do not be tempted to purchase a bag of relatively inexpensive brown nuts from a pet shop; these are intended to give the heavy beaks of parrots a good workout. Instead, you can find shelled pine nuts in health food stores or in the specialty section of supermarkets.

Pomegranates

This orange-size fruit has a tough red skin and thick yellow membranes to protect the delectable crimson jelly–covered seeds inside that are used whole in salsas or crushed into juice. Cut pomegranates into quarters, then peel back the membranes to free the seeds. Sometimes seeds fall out in clumps; delicately separate the individual seeds before use. While most people enjoy the gel surrounding the seeds, some do not like the small white seeds themselves. Alas, I know of no other way, other than juicing, to eliminate the white seeds in salsa.

Starfruit

Also known as *carambola*, this oblong fruit with five unusual ridges forms a star shape when cut widthwise. Starfruit are 2-to 4-inches long and vary from pale yellow-green to rich golden yellow depending on the season and the degree of ripeness. These are not skinned before using. The flavor is similar to citrus and ranges from very sweet to somewhat tart. While a star-shaped section is very pretty and should be kept intact for salsa toppings, dipping salsas require that each of the five points be cut off to make a 1/4- to 1/2-inch segment.

Tomatoes

Green, red, and yellow tomatoes, plus the little green-skinned husked tomatoes called *tomatillos*, are all utilized in salsa recipes. Here are some guidelines:

CHERRY TOMATOES: sweet, approximately 1 inch in diameter, with lots of juice and seeds. Should be cut into quarters or eighths, then seeded for uncooked salsa unless the fruit is very firm and not runny. For cooked salsa simply cut in half and remove the seeds if specified.

GREEN TOMATOES: unripe garden-variety tomatoes usually range from 2 to 4 inches in diameter and have an even balance of seeds and juice to meaty ribs. Firmer and less sweet than ripened or red tomatoes, they are not as tart as tomatillos, so they complement many salsa recipes. Used in combination with ripe tomatoes, they add more definition and complex flavor, and should be seeded. Some cooks insist on blanching the tomatoes to remove their skins before making salsa; I consider this unnecessary unless the skin is exceedingly thick. Most store-bought green tomatoes have thin skins.

PLUM TOMATOES, ALSO KNOWN AS ITALIAN, ITALIAN PLUM, AND ROMA TOMATOES: red oblong tomatoes about 1 1/2 inches in diameter and 3-inches long.

They are very firm when ripe and possess fewer seeds and less liquid than other varieties. Their skin is very thin and is not removed when making salsa. Their robust taste and meaty texture make them a wonderful choice for any recipe in this book; simply substitute two plum tomatoes for a medium tomato.

RED TOMATOES: ripe, garden-variety tomatoes come in three basic sizes; small (2 inches in diameter), medium (3 inches in diameter), and large (4 inches in diameter). Beefsteak tomatoes, which often reach 6 inches in diameter and can weigh over a pound, are too water retentive and bland to make exceptional salsa and are not preferred. It is best to buy tomatoes that are almost ripe, then let them ripen naturally on a sunny windowsill for several days before use. Tomatoes should be seeded, although skins do not need to be removed unless the fruit is especially thick-skinned. Use the most flavorful tomatoes you can find even if you have to grow them yourself, for a sensational salsa depends on bold, sweet, tasty tomatoes.

TOMATILLOS, ALSO KNOWN AS HUSK TOMATOES: range from 1 1/2 to 2 1/2 inches in diameter and are completely or partially covered in a wrinkly paperlike husk. This husk must be removed and the tomatillo washed thoroughly in soapy water prior to use in order to eliminate the clear, waxy residue that clings to the skin; make sure to rinse well and pat dry. These tart fruits with minuscule seeds do not need to be removed when used in uncooked or cooked salsa. Dice tomatillos as directed for uncooked salsa; half or quarter each fruit for cooked salsa.

YELLOW TOMATOES: are sometimes found in supermarkets but are mostly a home-grown product. These tomatoes are harvested halfway on their way to ripeness. Not as tart as completely green tomatoes, yet they lack the sweet juiciness of red ones. They are to be considered as a filler rather than a dominant flavor in salsa and should be used only in conjunction with either completely unripe or ripe tomatoes.

UNCOOKED SALSAS

AI CARAMBA CARIBE SALSA

Good for the beginning chile aficionado! This recipe yields a memorable experience—unless, that is, you forget fried taste buds quickly! Marinate meat or poultry in it before barbecuing, slather it on steaks or chicken breast while grilling, or serve it as a side dish, part of a festive Latin buffet spread.

1 medium red onion, finely diced

3/4 cup red wine vinegar

2 cups canned Italian tomatoes, drained

6 tablespoons chile caribe powder (or substitute red pepper flakes)

1 teaspoon oregano

1/2 teaspoon salt

1/2 teaspoon cumin

Place the onion in a medium bowl and cover with the vinegar. Let marinate 1 hour. In a separate bowl crush the tomatoes using the back of a fork. Stir the chile caribe powder, oregano, salt, and cumin into the tomatoes, whipping the mixture into a smoothly blended pulp. Pour the pulp into the onion-vinegar mixture and stir well. Cover and refrigerate for at least 1 hour to allow the flavors to merge. Allow to come to room temperature before serving.

Makes about 1 1/2 cups

APRICOT-PECAN SALSA

This glorious golden-orange relish goes great with ham. You may also want to try substituting an equal amount of diced apple for the jícama, doubling the amount of maple syrup, and pouring it over pancakes or French toast.

8 apricots, peeled, pitted, and cut into 1/4-inch cubes
1 orange, peeled, membranes removed, seeded, and finely diced
1/2 cup finely diced jícama
1/4 cup finely chopped pecans
1 jalapeño chile, seeded and minced
2 tablespoons maple syrup
2 teaspoons raspberry vinegar
2 teaspoons lemon juice

Combine all ingredients in a medium bowl. Serve at room temperature or microwave for 30 seconds on high for a warm salsa. It can be stored for up to 24 hours in the refrigerator.

Makes about 2 cups

AUTHENTIC SALSA CRUDA

This salsa is quickly prepared since the ingredients are roughly chopped and tossed together. It's extremely versatile and can be used as a chip dip, a condiment for barbecued meats, or layered into tacos and burritos.

2 large tomatoes, seeded and chopped
1 medium-size white onion, chopped
2 green onions (scallions), chopped
1 jalapeño chile, diced
2 tablespoons chopped cilantro
2 teaspoons fresh lime juice
1/2 teaspoon salt

Combine all the ingredients in a small bowl, stirring well. Serve immediately at room temperature or store in the refrigerator. It can be stored up to 2 days in the refrigerator.

Makes about 2 cups

AVOCADO-SHRIMP SALSA

"The sunbeams stream forward, dawn boys, with shimmering shoes of yellow." These words from a Mescalero Apache song remind me of the myriad pleasures of Arizona's endless summer: sunbathing, pool parties, and outdoor barbecues. At Casa PJ these three activities are often combined. But instead of humdrum hamburgers or hot dogs, featured entrees can range from grilled halibut to marinated free-range chicken breasts. Since some of my guests are not as captivated by capsicums (peppers) as I am, I created this refreshingly light salsa using no chiles. It's a colorful, dressy topping for plain broiled fish or grilled ham steaks and boasts plenty of flavor but no heat.

2 avocados, peeled, seeded, and cut into 1/2-inch chunks

1 cup cooked baby popcorn shrimp

2 green onions (scallions), finely diced

1 carrot, grated

1/4 cup watercress leaves

2 tablespoons fresh lime juice

1 tablespoon canola oil

1/2 teaspoon garlic salt

1/2 teaspoon lemon pepper

Mix all the ingredients together in a large bowl, being careful not to bruise the avocado. Serve immediately.

Makes about 2 cups

BANANA-COCONUT SALSA

I don't like using bananas in salsa because they turn brown and get mushy, but since they are in such constant supply, it seems a shame not to create at least a few recipes that include this fruit. This salsa uses other kitchen staples, plus shredded coconut, to create a tempting topping for shellfish dishes.

2 barely ripe bananas, peeled and cut into 1/4-inch cubes
1/4 cup finely shredded unsweetened coconut
1/4 small red bell pepper, seeded and diced into 1/4-inch cubes
1 jalapeño chile, seeded and minced
2 tablespoons slivered almonds
2 teaspoons minced cilantro
1 teaspoon maple syrup
1 teaspoon sesame oil
1 teaspoon fresh lime juice
1/2 teaspoon cinnamon
1/4 teaspoon ground cloves

Very gently combine the bananas, coconut, bell pepper, chile and almonds in a medium bowl. Combine the remaining ingredients in a small bowl, mixing well. Pour the liquid over the banana mixture and toss gently to coat. Serve immediately. This salsa will not keep.

Makes about 1 1/2 cups

CAN'T BE BEET SALSA

Forget those limp, sad-looking canned beets and go for the gusto with this vibrant-tasting salsa that's a winner when paired with roast poultry or pork. You can also spoon this salsa over a tossed green salad for added interest.

4 medium beets, peeled and finely grated

1/2 large red onion, cut into 1/4-inch cubes

4 tablespoons frozen orange juice concentrate, thawed

1 tablespoon grated orange zest

1 teaspoon sugar

1 teaspoon fresh lemon juice

1/2 teaspoon chili powder

1/2 teaspoon ground cloves

Combine the beets and onion in a medium bowl. Mix the remaining ingredients together well. Pour the liquid over the vegetables and stir well to coat. Serve immediately or cover and refrigerate up to 1 week. This salsa should not be heated.

Makes about 2 cups

CARIBE SALSA

Tiny caribe chiles are extremely hot, so adjust this recipe according to tolerance, if necessary. They are rarely sold fresh outside of New Mexico, so look for dried crushed caribe chiles to make this richly flavorful salsa. If necessary you can substitute dried crushed red pepper flakes, but the end result will lack the aromatics and heat that characterizes this recipe. The finished salsa is the perfect consistency for basting roasted chicken or barbecued beefsteak but can also be stirred into soup, stew, or spaghetti sauce to add firepower.

4 medium tomatoes, quartered

1/4 cup chile caribe powder

2 cloves garlic, minced

1 tablespoon dried oregano

1 teaspoon garlic salt

Place all the ingredients in a blender and process at medium speed until smooth. If the paste seems too thick, add 1 teaspoon of water at a time until the preferred consistency is reached. Serve immediately or cover and refrigerate up to 2 weeks.

Makes about 1 1/2 cups

CERVEZA SALSA

I've seen variations on this basic recipe for as long as I've been exploring dusty desert back roads. Where it originally came from, I don't know, but the tales are fascinating! I've been told about galavanting cowboys, inebriated frat pledges, desperate *pistoleros*, innovative bandito camp followers, and tipsy chuck wagon chefs. This juicy version is a wonderful chip dip or steak or pasta topping.

2 large tomatoes, seeded and cut into 1/2-inch cubes

2 serrano chiles, minced

1/2 medium red onion, cut into 1/4-inch cubes

2 cloves garlic, minced

1/4 cup chopped cilantro

3 tablespoons beer

1/2 tablespoon balsamic vinegar

1 teaspoon white wine vinegar

1 teaspoon olive oil

Combine all the ingredients in a medium bowl, tossing well. Serve immediately.

Makes about 2 1/2 cups

CHILE-FREE TOMATO SALSA

For those who like the consistency and combination of flavors in salsa but can't stand the heat, this chile-free creation will become a fabulous find. This salsa is versatile and can be served alongside tortilla chips, used to enhance a tossed green salad, or spooned over virtually any meat, poultry, or fish.

4 medium tomatoes, seeded and cut into 1/2-inch cubes

1/2 small yellow onion, chopped

2 green onions (scallions), diced

1 medium green bell pepper, seeded and chopped

1/2 cup chopped parsley

2 tablespoons apple cider vinegar

2 tablespoons honey

1 tablespoon fresh lime juice

1 tablespoon chopped Mexican oregano leaves

1/4 teaspoon mustard seed

1/4 teaspoon celery seed

1/4 teaspoon garlic salt

1/4 teaspoon lemon pepper

Mix all the ingredients thoroughly in a medium bowl. Cover and place in the refrigerator to marinate for 3 hours. Bring the salsa to room temperature before serving.

Makes about 3 cups

CITRUS-MINT SALSA

Fire and ice meet and merge in this intriguing salsa that's wonderful with baked halibut, roasted leg of lamb, or barbecued pork loin. Those wishing for less firepower should remove both seeds and ribs from the chile.

1 orange, peeled, membranes removed, seeded, and sectioned
1 small tart green apple, peeled, cored, and diced
2 serrano chiles, diced
1/2 cup fresh whole mint leaves
2 tablespoons fresh lemon juice
3 fresh whole mint leaves for garnish

Place all of the ingredients except the 3 whole mint leaves in a blender and process on medium speed until velvety smooth. Pour into a small dish and garnish with the mint leaves. Serve immediately.

Makes about 1 cup

CITRUS-PIQUIN SALSA

Tomatoes benefit when enhanced with citrus zip in this salsa suitable for topping any plainly cooked white-fleshed fish or spaghettini. When crushed and used fresh, the tiny green piquin chile has a violent heat that diminishes rapidly.

2 large tomatoes, seeded and cut into 1/2-inch cubes
1/2 grapefruit, peeled, seeded, and cut into 1/2-inch pieces
Juice of 1/2 grapefruit
1 tablespoon grated orange zest
2 green onions (scallions), finely diced
1/4 medium red onion, diced
1 piquin chile, crushed into tiny pieces

Combine all the ingredients in a medium bowl. Refrigerate overnight prior to serving. It can be stored in the refrigerator up to 2 days.

Makes about 3 cups

CITRUS SALSA

Swordfish tastes best when grilled outdoors over authentic mesquite charcoal briquettes, even those with smoke flavor added, cannot imitate the unique subtleties that real wood imparts to the firm white flesh of this delectable fish. Bright, tangy citrus salsa adds eye appeal as well as a clean, invigorating taste that goes perfectly with fish or broiled chicken breasts.

1/4 cup honey

1/8 cup fresh orange juice

2 tablespoons fresh lemon juice

1 teaspoon fresh black pepper

2 ruby grapefruits, peeled, sectioned, and cut into 1/2-inch pieces

2 oranges, peeled, sectioned, and cut into 1/2-inch pieces

1 tangerine, peeled, sectioned, and cut into 1/2-inch pieces

3 green onions (scallions), finely diced

12 cherry tomatoes, quartered

In a small bowl thoroughly mix together the honey, orange juice, lemon juice, and pepper until it has a smooth, thick consistency. Set aside. In a large bowl combine the remaining ingredients carefully so as not to crush the fruit pieces. Cover with the honey dressing and stir twice to combine. Cover the large bowl with plastic wrap and refrigerate until ready to use, up to 3 days.

Makes about 3 1/2 cups

CRUNCHY JÍCAMA SALSA

This savory-spicy salsa can be used to top salad greens, as a chip dip, or served alongside virtually any grilled or baked meat or poultry.

1/2 cup red wine vinegar

2 tablespoons light olive oil

2 cloves garlic, minced

1/4 cup chopped cilantro

2 tablespoons lemon zest

1/2 teaspoon crushed red pepper flakes

1/4 teaspoon fresh ground pepper

1 medium jícama (approximately 1lb.), peeled and cut into 1/2-inch cubes

2 celery stalks, finely diced

2 carrots, peeled and sliced into thin rounds

1 yellow bell pepper, stemmed, seeded, and cut into 1/2-inch pieces

1 zucchini, sliced into thin rounds

1 jalapeño chile, stemmed, seeded, and finely diced

In a small bowl combine the vinegar, oil, garlic, cilantro, lemon zest, and red pepper flakes. Set aside. Toss the remaining ingredients together in a large bowl. Pour the dressing over the vegetables, cover with plastic wrap, and refrigerate for 2 hours or overnight.

Makes about 3 cups

DRUNKEN BERRY SALSA

Luscious liqueur adds dimension to this "seedy" blend of fresh berries that is delightful when ladled over fish before baking or after poaching (especially salmon). Do not try pairing it with sautéed, grilled, or fried entrees; while it may sound tempting, do not pair this with desserts. If fresh cranberries are unavailable, thaw frozen berries just before use. And if you tipple in too much liqueur, you may find yourself up the Niagara without a paddle; a little does it.

1/2 cup halved blackberries
1/3 cup raspberries, halved only if the berries are large
1/3 cup cranberries
1 shallot, minced
1 clove garlic, minced
1 serrano chile, seeded and minced
2 tablespoons Chambord (blackberry) liqueur
1 tablespoon orange honey (or regular honey if necessary)
1 teaspoon raspberry vinegar

In a small bowl combine the berries, shallot, garlic, and chile. In a small bowl mix together the liqueur, honey, and vinegar (adding additional vinegar to taste, if desired). Pour the vinegar mixture over the berries, tossing gently to coat. Use immediately or cover and refrigerate.

Makes 1 to 1 1/4 cups

FRESH BASIL SALSA

This is a spicier version of tomato-basil spaghetti sauce, great for chip dipping, spooning over cheese pizza, or topping plain fettuccine. This chunky salsa can be pureed in a blender and then cooked in another tablespoon of oil for five minutes, stirring constantly, for a superior pasta sauce.

2 large tomatoes, seeded and cut into 1/4-inch cubes

1/2 small yellow onion, finely diced

1/4 cup chopped fresh basil leaves

1 serrano chile, minced

1 tablespoon walnut oil (or olive oil)

1 teaspoon white wine vinegar or champagne vinegar

1/2 teaspoon lemon juice

1/4 teaspoon dry mustard

1/4 teaspoon garlic salt

1/4 teaspoon lemon pepper

Combine the tomatoes, onion, basil leaves, and chile in a medium bowl. Mix together the oil, vinegar, lemon juice, and spices in a small bowl, then pour over the vegetables. Toss gently to coat and serve immediately, or process the salsa in a blender and cook it in another tablespoon of walnut oil for 5 minutes, as suggested above. This salsa will keep for 3 to 5 days in the refrigerator.

Makes about 2 cups

GREEN TOMATO SPRING SALSA

"As my eyes search the prairie, I feel the summer in the spring." These words from a Chippewa song describe the very moment when green tomatoes are at their flavorful best. This salsa was inspired by a visit to Sonora, Mexico, where I met a Papago tribal woman whose parents had migrated there from the almost three million acres of reservation land in southern Arizona. She told me that tomatoes are often harvested green in Mexico due to the lack of bountiful spring rains. This salsa complements grilled beef, duck, and chicken.

1/2 pound medium green tomatoes, roughly chopped

2 serrano chiles, seeded and chopped

1/2 small yellow onion, chopped

1 garlic clove, minced

1/2 cup chopped parsley

1/4 cup water

1 teaspoon brown sugar

1/2 teaspoon freshly ground pepper

1/4 teaspoon thyme

Place all the ingredients in a blender on medium speed and process just until smooth. If the texture is too pulpy, add additional water a half teaspoon at a time until the salsa is evenly blended but not liquefied. Pour into a bowl and serve immediately, or cover and refrigerate up to 1 week.

Makes about 1 cup

HEAVENLY HABANERO SALSA

The habanero is the world's hottest chile—more than one hundred times hotter than the jalapeño. I managed to survive my first encounter with a habanero chile during a visit to the Jicarilla reservation high in the mountains of northern New Mexico. This particular tribal offshoot of the Apache received their name from some Spanish explorers who identified the nomadic people by their pitch-lined drinking baskets. I could have used an oversized drinking bucket filled with milk after sampling the hair-raising habanero! This salsa spices up spaghetti sauce, perks up pizza, or—if you're really brave—can be enjoyed with chips.

2 large tomatoes, seeded and cut into 1/2-inch cubes
1 small red onion, finely chopped
1 habanero chile, seeded and minced
1/2 cup watercress leaves
1 teaspoon fresh lime juice
1/2 teaspoon lemon pepper

Place all the ingredients in a small bowl and mix well. Serve immediately or cover and store in the refrigerator.

Makes about 2 cups

KRAZY FOR KUMQUATS SALSA

The kumquat, a tangy tropical fruit, may have a funny name, but its unique flavor is unforgettable, especially when combined with the ingredients listed below. Serve this salsa alongside chicken, turkey, pork roast, or fish.

1 cup kumquats, seeded and cut into 1/4-inch cubes
1 serrano chile, seeded and minced
1 tablespoon minced red bell pepper
1 tablespoon minced cilantro
1 teaspoon orange juice
1 teaspoon pomegranate seeds (optional)

Mix all the ingredients together in a small bowl and serve immediately. The salsa can be covered and refrigerated up to 2 days.

Makes 1 1/4 cups

LAZY MAN'S SALSA

Too tired to chop tomatoes, chiles, and onions, but you want something to pour over that hurried lunch hamburger besides ketchup? Try this slothful sauce intended for the indolent. It can also be poked at by potato chips, meandered over meats, or laggardly stirred into lentils.

1 14-ounce can whole tomatoes, drained
1 4-ounce can diced mild green chiles
1 clove garlic
Salt and pepper to taste, if you have the gumption

Place all the ingredients in a blender and process until almost smooth. Can be stored in the refrigerator up to 1 week.

Makes about 1 cup

MOROCCAN OLIVE-ORANGE SALSA

While Spanish or Californian black olives and Florida oranges can be substituted, the listed ingredients combine in a way that makes this exotic salsa irresistible. It goes great with roasted lamb shank and braised eggplant. You can even spoon it on top of butter lettuce for a refreshing salad!

2 blood oranges, peeled, membranes removed, seeded, cut into 1/4-inch cubes

1/2 cup Moroccan olives, pitted and cut into 1/4-inch cubes

2 green onions (scallions), very finely diced

1 tablespoon fresh lemon juice

1/2 teaspoon ground cumin

1/2 teaspoon garlic salt

1/2 teaspoon cayenne pepper or chile caribe

Gently combine the oranges, olives, and onions in a small bowl. Mix the remaining ingredients well in a separate small bowl. Pour the liquid over the fruit and vegetables, tossing gently to combine. Serve immediately or cover and refrigerate up to 3 days. Salsa is best when served at room temperature.

Makes 1 to 1 1/4 cups

NOPALE-TOMATO SALSA

This chunky cactus pad salsa can be served with chips or crudites, but I prefer to stir it into chicken broth for an enticing soup or spoon it into quesadillas.

1 medium nopale, cut into 1/4-inch cubes

2 large tomatoes, seeded and cut into 1/2-inch cubes

2 green onions (scallions), finely chopped

2 tablespoons red wine vinegar

1 tablespoon canola oil

1 teaspoon fresh lime juice

1 teaspoon fresh thyme leaves or 1/2 teaspoon dry thyme leaves

1/4 teaspoon lemon pepper

1/4 teaspoon garlic salt

Combine the nopale, tomatoes, and onions in a large bowl. Set aside. Combine the remaining ingredients in a small bowl, stirring well. Pour the dressing over the salsa and toss gently. Use immediately or cover and refrigerate. Salsa should be used within 48 hours or the cactus will become limp.

Makes about 2 1/2 cups

OIL-FREE AVOCADO SALSA

Ripe, pebbly-skinned Haas avocados have a firm mouth feel and a rich buttery taste. Crisp cucumbers make a nice texture counterpoint, while red onion adds a pungent note to this easy-to-make, oil-free concoction. Serve it with a bowl of wedge-shaped blue and yellow corn tortilla chips and let guests help themselves, salsa-style, or portion it on top of mixed greens for a refreshing salad.

4 large avocados, peeled, pitted, and cut into 1-inch cubes

2 large cucumbers, peeled and cut into 1/2-inch cubes

2 large tomatoes, cored, seeded, and cut into 1/2-inch cubes

1/2 small red onion, cut into wafer-thin rings

3 cloves garlic, minced

2 teaspoons fresh lemon juice

1 teaspoon fresh lime juice

1 teaspoon fresh ground pepper

1 teaspoon chili powder

In a large bowl gently toss the avocados, cucumbers, tomatoes, and onion together. Mix the remaining ingredients together in a small bowl and then pour it over the avocado mixture. Cover the large bowl with plastic wrap and refrigerate for 1 hour before serving. Do not store overnight because avocados do not keep well and tend to brown.

Makes 3 1/2 to 4 cups

PAPAYA-PEPPER SALSA

The Mayans of ancient Mexico created a calendar that measured time over a million years. But don't worry; this inspired salsa can be made in minutes! A citrus undertone makes it a lovely topping for grilled ahi tuna, ono (sunfish), or New Zealand moki, a plump white-fleshed fish that is similar in taste to swordfish.

1 large papaya, peeled, split, seeded, and cut into 1/4-inch cubes

1/4 small red bell pepper, seeded and cut into 1/4-inch cubes

1/4 small green bell pepper, seeded and cut into 1/4-inch cubes

1 serrano chile, seeded and minced

1 tablespoon minced cilantro

1 teaspoon fresh lemon juice

1 teaspoon orange juice

1/2 teaspoon crushed red pepper flakes

Combine all the ingredients in a medium bowl and serve immediately, or cover and refrigerate for 2 hours before serving. This salsa will keep for only 24 hours.

Makes 1 to 1 1/4 cups

PASSION FRUIT SALSA

Vibrant and fruity, this lighthearted salsa is the perfect complement to grilled poultry and barbecued pork, although I've been guilty of spooning it over sorbet for a midnight snack! If tangelos are out of season, substitute a large orange for sweeter salsa or two small tangerines for tarter salsa. A friend of mine adds 1/4 cup diced pineapple when making this, but I find it decreases the impact of the exotic passion fruit.

3 passion fruit, cut in half

1 serrano chile, seeded and minced

Juice of 1 lime

2 tablespoons chopped cilantro

1/4 canteloupe, seeded and cut into 1/4-inch cubes

1 tangelo, peeled, membranes removed, seeded, and finely diced

Scoop out the pulp from the passion fruit into a medium bowl. Add the chile, lime juice, and cilantro, and stir gently. Fold in the canteloupe and tangelo pieces. Serve immediately. Can be covered and refrigerated overnight, but it will lose some of its fresh bite.

Makes about 2 cups

PEAR-MANGO SALSA

Succulent slices of juicy mango are a favorite treat of the ravens who live around my home in northern Arizona. Within seconds of leaving out a platter, I can always count on seeing at least one big black bird hopping impatiently from branch to branch, usually screeching at me to hurry inside so it can gorge itself. Nearly all the local Native American tribes have stories featuring a mischievous raven whose curiosity and desire to exploit others inevitably gets the trickster into trouble. I have actually witnessed one wise old raven leading a younger bird to a hidden cache of pine nuts, just to keep it occupied so the wily patriarch could devour all the fruit by himself. This salsa is delightful with roasted rabbit or any poultry.

3 pears, peeled, cored, and cut into 1/2-inch cubes

1 mango, peeled, seeded, and cut into 1/2-inch cubes

1 4-ounce can diced mild green chiles, drained

2 tablespoons fresh lemon juice

2 tablespoons minced parsley

1 tablespoon sesame seeds

Mix all the ingredients together and serve immediately. This salsa should not be kept overnight because the pears will discolor.

Makes about 2 cups

PEPPERED PEAR-RASPBERRY SALSA

The heady contrast between spicy hot and sweet makes this unusual salsa a fascinating complement to roast fowl, especially duck. While any variety of pear can be used, the custardlike consistency of the Anjou makes it my preferred choice. Make sure the pears are just ripe when making this salsa; overripe fruit can turn to mush, while underripe pears are too grainy, resulting in an unpleasant gritty texture.

3 Anjou pears, peeled, cored, seeded, and cut into 1/4-inch cubes
3 serrano chiles, minced
1 cup sweet white wine
1/2 cup raspberry vinegar
Juice of 1 lime
1 pint fresh raspberries, with larger fruit cut in half if necessary
1 teaspoon finely grated fresh ginger
1/2 teaspoon crushed red pepper flakes

Place the pear pieces in a small, deep bowl. Add the chiles, wine, vinegar, and lime juice. Cover and refrigerate overnight. Drain and discard the marinade and chile pieces, reserving 2 tablespoons of liquid. Add the raspberries to the pear pieces. Mix together the reserved liquid, ginger, and pepper flakes in a small bowl. Pour the liquid over the fruit. Stir gently to coat, being careful not to bruise the fruit. Serve immediately or cover and refrigerate no more than 2 hours prior to use. This salsa will not keep.

Makes about 2 1/2 cups

PICO DE GALLO SALSA

You'll want to do more than pick and scratch through this lively salsa, whose Spanish name translates loosely as "rooster's beak." Use the hottest little red radishes that you can find to boost firepower. One friend adapted this recipe to include the incendiary Japanese *wasabi* radish paste! Because it's so perky, this salsa should be served with only the simplest of meat, fish and poultry dishes, as a chip or vegetable dip, or spooned over rice, pasta, or spaghetti squash.

2 medium tomatoes, seeded and cut into 1/2-inch cubes

1 small red onion, cut into 1/4-inch cubes

6 small to medium red radishes, cut into 1/4-inch cubes

1 serrano chile, seeded and minced

2 jalapeño chiles, seeded and cut into 1/4-inch pieces

1 pasilla chile, seeded and cut into 1/4-inch pieces

1/2 cucumber, peeled, seeded, and cut into 1/4-inch cubes

1/2 cup chopped cilantro

1 tablespoon fresh lime juice

1 tablespoon fresh lemon juice

1 teaspoon red wine vinegar

1/2 teaspoon garlic salt

1/2 teaspoon lemon pepper

Combine the tomatoes, onion, radishes, chiles, cucumber, and cilantro in a medium bowl. Mix the remaining ingredients well in a small bowl. Pour the liquid over the vegetables and toss gently to coat. Serve immediately or cover and refrigerate. This salsa is best when made and used fresh.

Makes about 2 1/2 cups

PICKLE SALSA

This salsa is the perfect relish for hot dogs and hamburgers but can also be slathered inside a grilled cheese sandwich or a B.L.T.

2 medium tomatoes, seeded and cut into 1/2-inch cubes

1 large peach, peeled, pitted, and cut into 1/4-inch cubes

1/4 cup finely diced white onion

1 large whole sweet pickle, cut into 1/4-inch cubes

3 tablespoons apple cider vinegar

1 teaspoon clover honey

1 teaspoon fresh lime juice

1 teaspoon whole pickling spice

Mix all the ingredients in a large bowl. Cover and let marinate in the refrigerator for 24 hours. This salsa is best served at room temperature and should not be heated. It can be stored in the refrigerator for an additional 24 hours.

Makes about 2 cups

RAGIN' RED PEPPER-PIMIENTO SALSA

While driving through the Fort Apache reservation I saw a silversmith's booth and decided to stop. The turquoise jewelry was lovely but not as beautiful as the tale told to me by the proprietor. There was a time when all the animals talked like people, and a turkey overheard a boy begging his sister for food. When the turkey learned that the children had nothing to eat, he shook himself all over, and many kinds of wild fruits and vegetables dropped out from among his feathers. Besides blue oak acorns, pine nuts, sumac, and manzanita berries, a variety of peppers appeared, including the red bell pepper featured in the recipe below. This salsa complements roast beef and prime rib.

1 medium red bell pepper, seeded and cut into very thin 1-inch-long strips

1 7-ounce can diced pimientos, drained

1/4 cup sliced black olives

2 tablespoons canola oil

2 tablespoons apple juice

1 tablespoon honey

1/2 teaspoon lemon pepper

1/4 teaspoon crushed red pepper flakes

Combine all of the ingredients in a medium bowl, stirring well. Serve immediately or cover and refrigerate up to 2 days.

Makes about 1 1/2 cups

SALT-FREE SALSA

This blend of vegetables, fruits, and spices packs plenty of flavor without a bit of salt. Of course, those on a sodium-free diet can simply eliminate the salt or garlic salt called for in any of the recipes in this book, or an equal amount of salt substitute can be used. As a no-sodium alternative to the garlic salt called for in many recipes, you can use 3/4 teaspoon of salt substitute plus 1/4 teaspoon of granulated garlic to equal 1 teaspoon of garlic salt.

3 large tomatoes, quartered and seeded
1/3 cup frozen apple juice concentrate
1 tablespoon fresh lime juice
1 orange, peeled, membranes removed, seeded, sectioned, cut into 1/2-inch pieces
1/4 cup raisins
1 serrano chile, seeded and minced
1/2 teaspoon cinnamon
1/4 teaspoon cloves

Place the tomatoes, apple juice concentrate, and lime juice in a blender and process on high speed until smooth. Pour the mixture into a medium saucepan. Add the remaining ingredients and simmer for 20 minutes or until thick, stirring frequently. Serve immediately or cover and refrigerate up to 24 hours.

Makes about 1 1/2 cups

SASSY JÍCAMA SALSA

This exceedingly crunchy salsa is lightly sweet, making it a first-choice condiment for sliced cold chicken breast, barbecued pork tacos, or Asian pan-fried noodles. Stir in mayonnaise to taste for a chunky spread that spices up sandwiches! Half of a medium jícama will weigh approximately 7 to 9 ounces and resemble a large baking potato in shape.

1/2 medium jícama, peeled, washed well, patted dry, cut into 1/4-inch cubes

1 large cucumber, peeled, seeded, and cut into 1/2-inch cubes

2 tablespoons pineapple, cut into 1/4-inch cubes

1 tablespoon red pepper, cut into 1/4-inch cubes

1 tablespoon pineapple juice

1 teaspoon fresh lime juice

1/2 teaspoon chili powder

Combine the jícama, cucumber, pineapple, and red pepper in a medium bowl. Mix together the pineapple juice, lime juice, and chili powder in a small bowl. Pour the liquid over the jícama mixture and toss gently to coat. Serve immediately or cover and refrigerate up to 24 hours.

Makes 2 to 2 1/2 cups

SCINTILLATING SCALLION SALSA

Cumin adds an unexpected Middle Eastern flavor to this robust salsa. Serve it alongside beef or lamb kabobs and big bowls of yogurt-marinated cucumber slices.

2 medium green tomatoes, seeded and cut into 1/4-inch cubes

4 green onions (scallions), finely diced

1/4 cup finely diced white onion

2 tablespoons finely chopped parsley

1 serrano chile, seeded and minced

1 teaspoon cumin

1 teaspoon olive oil

1 teaspoon fresh lemon juice

1 teaspoon rice wine vinegar

Combine all the ingredients in a medium bowl. Serve immediately or cover and refrigerate up to 3 days.

Makes about 1 1/2 cups

SIMPLE SALSA

This versatile and extremely basic recipe can be served chunky as a salsa or placed in a blender and processed on high speed for a velvet-textured hot sauce. Broiling the tomatoes prior to blending will add a smoky undertone to the processed sauce. Spoon the salsa over tacos, quesadillas, or tostada salad. Shake the hot sauce over steaks, burgers, even french fries; it's a spicy alternative to ketchup.

2 large tomatoes, seeded and cut into 1/4-inch cubes
1/4 cup finely diced yellow onion
2 serrano chiles, minced
1 clove garlic, minced
1/4 teaspoon garlic salt

For salsa: Combine all the ingredients in a small bowl and serve immediately.

Makes about 1 1/4 cups

For sauce: Place all the ingredients in a blender and process on high speed until smooth. Warm 2 tablespoons of canola oil in a medium saucepan over high heat. Pour into the blended sauce and cook for 4 minutes, stirring constantly, or until the sauce begins to thicken. Remove from the heat, let cool, and serve. The sauce can be covered and refrigerated up to 1 week.

Makes about 1 cup

SNAZZY SALSA FRESCA

This medium-hot salsa makes a great chip dip or a spicy condiment for hamburgers and chopped sirloin steak. Dice the tomatoes, onion, and peppers in equal-sized 1/2-inch pieces for the best effect. Around here, this recipe reeks of *haute cuisine*, which a local chef told me means "cooking high." Mmm, is that *really* Mexican oregano, or ...?

2 large tomatoes, seeded and diced

1/2 medium red onion, diced

4 serrano chiles, seeded and diced

2 teaspoons fresh lime juice

1 teaspoon oregano (Mexican preferred)

1/2 teaspoon garlic salt

Mix all the ingredients well in a small bowl. Cover and place in the refrigerator to marinate for 2 hours. Bring the salsa to room temperature prior to serving. This salsa will not keep.

Makes about 2 1/2 cups

SOLID GOLD SALSA

Cheerful to look at, nifty to nosh, this versatile salsa can be used as a chip or vegetable dip, spooned over simple grilled meats or poultry, or used as a soup garnish. Gold tequila (pronounced teh-KEEL-ya, as in you have too much and you keel over) can be added, but limit the amount used to under one tablespoon.

1 pint yellow cherry tomatoes, cut into eighths
1/3 cup finely diced yellow or Bermuda onion
1 shallot, minced
1 pasilla chile, seeded and minced
2 tablespoons orange juice
1 tablespoon sesame oil
1 teaspoon white pepper
1 teaspoon minced fresh basil leaves

Combine the tomatoes, onion, shallot, and chile in a medium bowl. Mix the remaining ingredients together in a small bowl. Pour the liquid over the vegetables and toss gently to coat. Serve immediately or cover and refrigerate up to 3 days.

Makes about 1 1/2 cups

SPICED MIXED MELON SALSA

There are many delicious melons on the market to choose from, so feel free to substitute musk for canary, canteloupe for crenshaw. This versatile salsa is delicious when spooned over homemade fruit sorbet or vanilla ice cream. It can also be poured over the top of a whole roasted chicken approximately thirty minutes before the fowl is completely cooked. For a thicker glaze, add 1/2 cup brown sugar and double the amount of pineapple.

1/2 cup raisins
1/2 crenshaw melon, split, seeded, and scooped into 1/2-inch balls
1/2 honeydew melon, split, seeded, and scooped into 1/2-inch balls
1/2 canary melon, split, seeded, and scooped into 1/2-inch balls
1 cup pineapple chunks, with their juice
1 4-ounce can diced jalapeño chiles, drained

Place the raisins in a small heat-resistant bowl and cover with boiling water. Let soak for 30 minutes or until plumped. Drain the water and discard. Pour the raisins into a large bowl and combine with the remaining ingredients, stirring gently to mix well without bruising the melon pieces. Serve immediately or cover and refrigerate up to 2 days.

Makes 2 to 2 1/2 cups

SUMMER FRUIT SALSA

Hot and sweet, this brightly colored dessert salsa dresses up homemade ice cream flavored with Mexican vanilla, avocado sorbet, or sponge cake. It is important that the fruit and chile pieces be cut in the same-sized small pieces, ensuring that the disparate flavors can be enjoyed equally with every bite. Just keep working your *burro* off, and you'll get it.

1/2 cup strawberries, stemmed and cut into 1/4-inch cubes

1 guava, peeled, seeded, and cut into 1/4-inch cubes

1 papaya, peeled, seeded, and cut into 1/4-inch cubes

2 serrano chiles, seeded, and cut into 1/4-inch cubes

1 tablespoon pine nuts

2 tablespoons Cointreau or Triple Sec

1 tablespoon sugar

1/2 teaspoon freshly ground pepper (optional)

Combine the fruit, chiles, and pine nuts in a medium bowl. Mix the liqueur, sugar, and pepper together in a small bowl, making sure the sugar dissolves. Pour the sweetened liqueur over the fruit and toss gently to combine. Serve immediately or cover and refrigerate up to 3 hours and serve cold. This salsa is not at its best when eaten the next day.

Makes about 1 1/2 cups

SUSHI SALSA

My friends visiting from southern California invariably fall in love at first bite with Arizona's regional cuisine. After sampling a variety of my homemade salsas, they usually end up asking for a recipe that complements the raw fish dishes popular along the sun-drenched coastal communities, particularly sushi and sashimi. I decided to experiment with Asian ingredients in the hope of finding a suitable side dish; this is the result. As always, if you are making any meal that utilizes raw fish, make sure it is extremely fresh and clean.

1/2 cup finely grated carrot

1/4 cup finely grated daikon (a type of radish)

1/4 cucumber, peeled, seeded, and cut into 1/4-inch cubes

2 green onions (scallions), finely diced

1 tablespoon fresh lime juice

1 tablespoon tamari soy sauce

1/2 tablespoon sake (rice wine)

1 teaspoon finely grated fresh ginger

Combine the carrot, daikon, cucumber, and onions in a small bowl, mixing well. Mix the lime juice, tamari, sake, and ginger together in a small bowl. Pour the liquid over the vegetables and toss well to coat. Serve immediately or cover and chill for at least 2 hours to serve cold. It can be stored up to 3 days in the refrigerator.

Makes about 1 cup

TERRIFYING TURNIP SALSA

When her young children are misbehaving, a gal pal of mine threatens to make her offspring eat an entire bowl of this salsa...each! She tells me this works better than banning the Nintendo! But I have it from good authority (that is, her hubbie) that she secretly makes midnight raids on the refrigerator in order to indulge her private passion for this mouth-puckering delight. If in-season turnips are not available, feel free to substitute rutabagas; 2 medium turnips are the equivalent of 1/3 a medium rutabaga. Serve it alongside steamed cauliflower, squash, or another simple vegetable side dish.

2 medium turnips, peeled and cut into 1/4-inch cubes

1 large tart green apple, peeled, cored, seeded, and cut into 1/4-inch cubes

1/4 cup minced cilantro

2 tablespoons fresh lime juice

1 tablespoon tarragon oil

1/2 teaspoon chili powder

1/2 teaspoon freshly ground pepper

Combine the turnips, apple, and cilantro in a small bowl. Mix the remaining ingredients together in a small bowl. Pour the liquid over the turnip mixture, tossing gently to coat. Serve immediately; this salsa does not keep well.

Makes about 2 cups

TIJUANA PICO DE GALLO

This variation on traditional Rooster's Bill (Pico de Gallo) is sold as a "finger salad" by street vendors in Tijuana as well as up and down the beautiful Baja peninsula. If jícama is not available, you can substitute an equal amount of tart green apple; the texture will be similar, but the flavor will be less exotic. This goes great with fish dishes.

1 3/4 cups peeled jícama cut into 1/2-inch cubes

1 large orange, peeled, membranes removed, seeded, cut into 1/4-inch pieces

1/4 small red onion, cut into 1/4-inch cubes

2 tablespoons fresh lemon juice

1 teaspoon chili powder

1 teaspoon garlic salt

Combine the jícama, orange, and onion in a medium bowl. Mix the remaining ingredients together well in another bowl and pour it over the jícama mixture, tossing well to coat. Serve immediately or cover and refrigerate overnight prior to serving.

Makes about 2 cups

UPTOWN SALSA VERDE

I had been dying to do something special with anchovies, but the thought of mincing them was tiresome beyond belief. Here you get to enjoy the fabulous flavor of anchovies and capers without the work! This salsa is especially delicious drizzled over hot steamed vegetables. It can also be added to whipped potatoes or spooned over baked potatoes.

1 cup watercress leaves

1 cup chopped parsley

1/2 cup chopped cilantro

1 clove garlic, chopped

1 small white onion, chopped

2 anchovy fillets

3 tablespoons canola oil

2 tablespoons capers

2 tablespoons tarragon vinegar

1 teaspoon lime zest

1/2 teaspoon chile caribe or red pepper flakes

Place all the ingredients in a blender and process on medium speed just until smooth. Store in the refrigerator up to 1 week.

Makes about 1 cup

WATER CHESTNUT SALSA

Fresh water chestnuts, which possess a sweetness that is not present in their canned counterparts, can be obtained from any Asian produce market. If you must use canned, add 1/4 teaspoon of sugar to this recipe. The light, crunchy texture of this Oriental salsa is the perfect complement to pan-fried white fish, grilled scallops, or barbecued halibut. Note: Make sure to peel and wash fresh chestnuts before dicing; rinse canned chestnuts.

1 cup washed and diced water chestnuts (peeled if fresh)

1/4 cup slivered almonds

1 Hungarian wax chile, seeded and minced

1 tablespoon chopped pimiento

1 tablespoon toasted sesame seeds

1/2 teaspoon sesame oil

1/2 teaspoon rice wine vinegar

1 tablespoon fresh lemon juice

In a small bowl mix all the ingredients together except the lemon juice. Immediately before serving sprinkle the lemon juice over the salsa. This salsa should not be refrigerated and will not keep.

Makes about 1 1/2 cups

YIPEE YI YAM SALSA

According to the *Popol Vuh*, the sacred history of Central America's Quiche Maya (written in approximately 1000 A.D.), four kind-hearted animals—the mountain cat, the coyote, the crow, and a small parrot—brought food to the newly created and starving race of Man. Primary among the items that came to sustain the hungry people were corn, honey, cacao (from which chocolate comes), beans, and yams. The firm texture and sweetish flavor of the latter forms the basis for this unusual salsa; blistering jalapeños provide a compelling contrast of tastes. The salsa can be heated and then tossed with linguine, or it can be served as a side dish with baked turkey, chicken, or ham.

1 large tomato, seeded and cut into 1/2-inch cubes

1 medium yam, cooked (at 375°F for 45 minutes) cut into 1/2-inch cubes
(about 1 cup)

1 4-ounce can jalapeño chiles, drained and sliced

1/4 cup raisins

2 tablespoons honey

2 tablespoons fresh orange juice

Combine the tomato and yam in a medium bowl, mixing gently so as not to crush the yam pieces. Fold in the jalapeños and raisins. In a separate small bowl, whip the honey and orange juice together. Pour the dressing over the mixture and serve. This salsa can be heated in the microwave and served hot. It can be stored in the refrigerator up to 2 days.

Makes about 2 cups

COOKED
SALSAS

BLACKENED TOMATO-MINT SALSA

Mexican cooks use a *comal*, a stone griddle, to scorch the tomato skins without using oil, creating a rich, smoky undertone; a dry skillet works just as well, however. Smother chile rellenos with this sauce or spoon it over a macaroni and cheese casserole; this salsa can also be used instead of ketchup.

4 medium tomatoes

1 clove garlic, minced

2 tablespoons fresh lime juice

2 tablespoons canola oil

1/2 teaspoon chili powder

2 New Mexican long red chiles, seeded and finely diced

4 tablespoons chopped spearmint leaves

Blacken the whole tomatoes by placing them in a nongreased, preheated skillet over high heat and turning frequently until the skins are scorched. Roughly chop the tomatoes while they are still warm. Drain and discard the juice and most of the seeds. Place the tomatoes, garlic, lime juice, canola oil, and chili powder in a food processor and blend until smooth. Pour the puree into a small bowl, add the remaining ingredients, and mix thoroughly. Serve immediately, or cover and refrigerate up to 5 days; bring to room temperature before serving.

Makes about 2 cups

ANCHO-PEPPERCORN SALSA

This is a very thick, very smooth, complexly seasoned salsa that bastes roasted meat, such as prime rib, beautifully. It also accents duck rellenos, quail enchiladas, and rabbit cutlets with equal verve. Substitute chicken stock for beef broth if serving with poultry.

8 ancho chiles, roasted, skinned, seeded, and chopped

3 tablespoons chopped red onion

1 clove garlic, chopped

1/3 cup beef broth

1 teaspoon cracked black peppercorns

1 teaspoon sugar

1 teaspoon cinnamon

1/2 teaspoon nutmeg

1/2 teaspoon ground cloves

2 tablespoons canola oil

Place all the ingredients except the canola oil in a blender and process on low speed until fairly smooth. Heat the oil in a medium saucepan over high heat. Add the salsa and cook for 5 minutes, stirring constantly, or until the salsa becomes very thick. Remove from the heat and serve immediately. This salsa should be served hot.

Makes about 1 cup

ATTACK OF THE KILLER TOMATO SALSA

Like the huge man-eating vegetables of the B-movies, this salsa is big on taste and possesses a diabolical attitude. Your taste buds will receive no mercy from this hellish salsa that could be substituted for tomato sauce in virtually any recipe. Use it to wake up maudlin meatloaf, liven up lasagna, or pick up eggplant parmigiana.

10 medium tomatoes, seeded and quartered
1 habanero chile, seeded and diced
1 small yellow onion, diced
2 garlic cloves, diced
1 tablespoon sugar
1 tablespoon oregano (Mexican preferred)
1/4 teaspoon thyme
1/4 teaspoon marjoram
1/4 teaspoon rosemary
2 tablespoons canola oil

Place all the ingredients except the oil in a blender and process on high speed until smooth. Place the oil in a medium saucepan over medium heat. Add the sauce and cook for 6 to 8 minutes, stirring frequently, until the sauce has thickened. It can be stored in the refrigerator up to 1 week.

Makes about 3 cups

CHICKEN SOUP SALSA

Like that fabled cold remedy, this salsa is good for whatever ails you. I serve it alongside baked chicken, duck tamale pie, or stuffed acorn squash.

6 tomatillos, husked and washed well

6 Anaheim green chiles, roasted, skinned, seeded, and chopped

1 jalapeño chile, chopped and seeded

1/2 cup dry roasted peanuts

1 teaspoon garlic salt

1/2 teaspoon freshly ground pepper

1/4 teaspoon cayenne pepper

2 tablespoons canola oil

2/3 cup chicken stock

Bring 1 quart of water to a boil in a medium, deep pot over high heat. Add the tomatillos, lower the heat, and simmer for 15 minutes or until the tomatillos are soft. Drain and let the tomatillos cool. Cut the tomatillos into quarters and place in a blender with the remaining ingredients except for the canola oil and 1/3 cup of the chicken stock. Process the salsa on low speed until fairly smooth. Heat the oil in a medium saucepan over medium-high heat. Pour the contents of the blender into the saucepan and cook for 5 minutes, stirring constantly. Add the remaining chicken stock and bring the mixture to a boil over high heat for 1 minute, stirring constantly. Remove from the heat and pour into a serving bowl. Use immediately. This salsa should be served warm to hot.

Makes about 1 1/2 cups

CHIPOTLE SALSA VERDE

Whole dried chipotle chiles are difficult to find outside New Mexico; if you do find some, soak them in hot water for thirty minutes, then drain them before making this salsa. When using canned chipotles, make sure to utilize the rich smoky red sauce in which the chiles were packed. This salsa is best served with the simplest of grilled meat or poultry and uncluttered side dishes, such as steamed vegetables or rice.

1 large green tomato, seeded and cut into 1/2-inch-thick slices

Olive oil for brushing

1 4-ounce can chipotle chiles or 4 chiles if dried and rehydrated (see above)

1 small yellow onion, chopped

6 tomatillos, husked, washed well, and quartered

1 clove garlic, chopped

2 tablespoons pine nuts

1 tablespoon chopped parsley

1 teaspoon garlic salt

1 teaspoon lemon pepper

2 tablespoons canola oil

Preheat the broiler. Brush the green tomato slices with olive oil on both sides and arrange on an ungreased shallow baking pan. Place in the oven and broil approximately 4 inches away from the heating element for 1 to 2 minutes on each side or until black spots appear. Remove from the oven and place in a blender with the remaining ingredients except the canola oil. Process on medium speed until a fairly thick salsa has formed.

Heat the oil in a medium saucepan over medium-high heat. Add the salsa to the saucepan and cook for 4 to 5 minutes, stirring constantly, or until the sauce thickens. Remove from the heat and serve immediately. The salsa should be served warm to hot. It can be stored in the refrigerator up to 3 days.

Makes 1 1/2 to 2 cups

COOKED CILANTRO SALSA

Cilantro's soapy-lemon flavor is an acquired taste for some; other people can't make salsa without it. I use this salsa to top baked potatoes and steamed vegetables, and sometimes I mix it into rice pilaf.

1/4 cup unsalted butter
1 small yellow onion, finely chopped
1 clove garlic, minced
2 bunches cilantro, leaves only (approximately 1 1/2 cups)
1/4 teaspoon salt
1/4 teaspoon lemon pepper

Melt the butter in a medium skillet over medium-high heat. When it foams, add the onion and garlic, cooking until the onions turn clear. Lower the heat to medium and add the cilantro and seasonings. Cook, stirring constantly, until the butter is absorbed. Remove from the heat, place in a small bowl, and serve immediately, do not store.

Makes about 1 1/2 cups

DELIGHTFUL THREE-TOMATO SALSA

This cooked salsa was inspired by a condiment served at Enchantment, an elegant resort in the heart of Arizona's spectacular red rock country.

2 tablespoons canola oil

1/2 medium yellow onion, diced

1/4 yellow bell pepper, seeded and diced

1/4 red bell pepper, seeded and diced

2 tablespoons dry white wine

8 tomatillos, husked, washed well, and diced

2 large tomatoes, seeded and diced

1 pint yellow cherry tomatoes, halved

2 tablespoons cilantro

1/2 teaspoon dried fines herbes

1/2 teaspoon freshly ground pepper

1/4 teaspoon thyme

Heat the oil in a large skillet over medium-high heat. Add the onion and peppers and cook for 3 minutes, stirring frequently. Lower the heat to medium and add the wine and tomatillos. Cook for 1 minute, stirring constantly. Remove from the heat and add the remaining ingredients, stirring gently. Pour into a medium bowl, cover, and refrigerate for 2 hours. Use chilled or let warm to room temperature. It can be stored in the refrigerator up to 3 days.

Makes about 3 cups

EASY ENCHILADA SALSA

This cooked salsa is something I keep in the refrigerator at all times; it's so versatile! While not suitable for dips, it makes a wonderful ingredient for chili con carne, baked beans, or casserole. I've stirred small portions of it into rice, stew, and soup; I've even used it to flavor soufflés! And yes, you can pour it over enchiladas or any other Mexican fare with *flair!*

2 tablespoons unsalted butter

2 tablespoons flour

1 8-ounce can tomato paste

1 clove garlic, minced

1/4 small white onion, minced

1 tablespoon cornstarch

2 teaspoons chili powder

1 teaspoon freshly ground pepper

2 cups milk

Melt the butter in a medium saucepan over medium-high heat. Lower the heat to medium, add the flour, and, stirring constantly, make a smooth paste. Add the remaining ingredients except the milk, stirring until well blended. Slowly pour in the milk and continue cooking until the sauce thickens, about 3 minutes; stir constantly to make sure the sauce does not stick. Serve hot. Store in the refrigerator up to 1 week.

Makes about 2 cups

ENSENADA SALSA ROJA

While traveling in the hills above the seaport city of Ensenada, in Baja California, I met a retired olive rancher and his wife who invited me to share their simple dinner and allowed me to peek in the kitchen while preparations were going on. The peanut butter thickens and adds dimension to this salsa that should smother enchiladas or roast chicken with dumplings. I like to garnish such dishes with chopped dry-roasted peanuts after the salsa has been applied.

4 ancho chiles, blackened, peeled, and chopped

3 plum tomatoes, chopped

1 cup tomato juice

1/8 cup chunky peanut butter

1 clove garlic

1/2 teaspoon cinnamon

1/2 teaspoon allspice

1/2 teaspoon oregano

1/2 teaspoon freshly ground pepper

1/2 teaspoon garlic salt

1/4 teaspoon thyme

1/4 teaspoon marjoram

2 tablespoons peanut oil

Place all the ingredients except the oil in a blender and process on low speed until smooth. Heat the oil in a medium-size saucepan over medium-high heat, add the

salsa, and cook the salsa for 5 minutes, stirring constantly, or until the salsa thickens. Pour into a serving bowl and use immediately.

Makes about 1 cup

EPAZOTE SALSA ROJA

Like cilantro, epazote can be an acquired taste for some, but in this recipe the herb contributes an unusual flavor accent that is unmistakable. Ladle this warmed salsa over braised rabbit, Cornish game hens, or stuffed squab.

4 medium tomatoes, seeded and chopped
2 poblano chiles, blackened, skinned, and seeded
1/4 cup water
1/4 cup chopped red onion
4 tablespoons dried epazote leaves
1 teaspoon sugar
1 teaspoon garlic salt

Place all the ingredients in a blender and process on high speed until smooth, adding water a teaspoonful at a time until the desired consistency is achieved; I prefer it rather thick. Pour into a small saucepan and warm over low heat for 5 minutes, stirring occasionally. Pour into a small bowl and serve immediately.

Makes about 2 cups

FIVE BROTHERS SALSA

A quintet of capsicums is the basis of this tomatoless salsa. This creation is a perfect topping for steaks, grilled chicken breasts, or even broiled tempeh and marinated tofu.

4 tablespoons unsalted butter
1 medium yellow onion, diced
1/2 green bell pepper, seeded and cut into thin 1-inch-long strips
1/2 red bell pepper, seeded and cut into thin 1-inch-long strips
1 New Mexican green chile, roasted, skinned, seeded, cut into 1/2-inch pieces
2 Hungarian yellow wax chiles, seeded and diced
1 serrano chile, seeded and minced
2 teaspoons sugar
1 teaspoon fresh lime juice
1 teaspoon honey
1 teaspoon crushed red chile flakes

Melt the butter in a large frying pan over medium heat. When it foams, add the onion, bell peppers, and chiles. Sauté until tender, about 6 to 8 minutes, stirring frequently to avoid browning. Stir in the remaining ingredients, lower the heat, and simmer for 10 minutes, stirring occasionally, until a light glaze coats the peppers and a test piece of vegetable is almost soft. Serve immediately or refrigerate up to 1 week and then reheat. This salsa should be served warm.

Makes about 3 cups

GEHENNA'S OWN GINGER SALSA

Hotter than heck. There's no way around it, but the exotic heat of ginger combined with chiles makes for an unusual condiment for those who can't get enough flame in their flavor. Use it sparingly at first with dishes such as vegetable fettuccine, spinach soufflé, or moo goo gai pan. If your first attempt is too incendiary to tolerate, simply lessen the number of piquin chiles used until an acceptable level of spiciness is achieved.

6 piquin chiles, crushed

3 fresh green Oriental peppers, minced

1/2 medium yellow onion, diced

1/4 green pepper, seeded and diced

2 cups tomato sauce

1/4 cup grated fresh ginger

2 cloves garlic, chopped

1 teaspoon garlic salt

1 teaspoon lemon pepper

Place all the ingredients in a medium pot and bring to a boil over medium-high heat. Lower the heat and simmer for 15 to 18 minutes, stirring frequently. Remove from the heat and let cool to room temperature. Pour the mixture into a blender and process on medium speed until smooth. Serve immediately or cover and refrigerate for up to 1 week.

Makes about 1 1/2 cups

FLAMING PRICKLY PEAR SALSA

Prickly pears are favored by many desert-dwelling humans as well as the local Sedona, Arizona, *javelina* (a variety of wild boar). After two nights of placing a large bowl of dry dog food on the lawn, a small herd of sows and their wee piglets decided to sample this exotic new fare. The crunch-crunch-crunch of mighty boar teeth woke me around midnight, but seeing their smiling furry faces in the moonlight convinced me to continue feeding them when the pears were not in season.

Humans are luckier than *javelina* since fresh pears can be found in many supermarkets year-round. This snazzy salsa should be ladled on pork loin, boneless chicken breasts, Cornish game hens, or angel food cake, then set alight.

12 medium prickly pears

2 pears, peeled, cored, and cut into 1/2-inch cubes

2 tablespoons unsalted butter

2 tablespoons frozen orange juice concentrate

3 tablespoons fresh lemon juice

1/2 cup sugar

1/4 cup bottled or canned pomegranate juice

3/4 cup brandy

2 tablespoons flour

Place the prickly pears in a heat-resistant bowl and cover with boiling water. Let sit for 2 minutes, then drain. Using tongs, hold the individual fruits and remove the stickers with tweezers. Still using tongs, cut away the skin with a sharp paring knife.

Cut the peeled fruit in half lengthwise and scoop out the seeds with a small spoon; discard the seeds. Chop the fruit into 1/2-inch pieces and set aside. Melt the butter and orange juice concentrate in a medium skillet over medium heat. Add the lemon juice, sugar, prickly pears, and pears, and stir to blend. Add the pomegranate juice, 1/4 cup of the brandy, and flour, stirring well. Raise the heat to medium-high and let the mixture bubble for 2 minutes, stirring constantly. Remove the skillet from the heat and spoon the mixture over meat or cake on a prepared serving platter. Pour the remaining 1/2 cup of brandy over the fruit mixture. Ignite the mixture using a long-handled wooden match and serve, being careful of clothing and long hair. Let the flame burn out naturally or gently shake the platter until the flame dies.

Makes about 2 cups

HOT GARLIC SALSA

We return thanks to our mother, the earth, which sustains us;
We return thanks to the rivers and streams.
We return thanks to all herbs, which furnish medicines for the cure of
    our diseases.

—*Iroquois Prayer*

Of all the herbs and seasonings known to us, perhaps none has been honored as much as simple garlic. Historically it has been ingested as an aphrodisiac, a blood purifier, an insect repellant (though when my boyfriend eats too much, he ends up repelling me, too!), and an arthritis "cure," not to mention its mythic vampire discouraging properties. In recent times the potent bulb has grown so popular that numerous American cities devote week-long festivals to celebrating its outstanding qualities. Numerous newsletters and magazines are published quarterly, solely dedicated to promoting garlic consciousness. In this exuberant spirit I am pleased to offer a redolent recipe for true garlic aficionados. It can be spooned sparingly over steak, or used to spice up stews.

12 Hungarian wax chiles, washed, stemmed, seeded, and minced
1 serrano chile, washed, stemmed, seeded and minced
10 cloves garlic, minced
2 red-skinned radishes, minced
1 tablespoon crushed red pepper flakes
1/4 teaspoon garlic salt

Combine all the ingredients in a small microwave-safe bowl. Heat the salsa in a microwave oven prior to serving for no more than 30 seconds on the high setting. Serve immediately.

Makes about 1 cup

GRINGO SALSA VERDE

This is a very mild green sauce for tender taste buds. To sweeten the salsa, add one teaspoon of honey or one tablespoon of orange juice during the blending process.

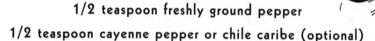

3 large green tomatoes, finely chopped

2 tomatillos, husked, washed well, and chopped

1 small yellow onion, finely diced

3/4 cup apple cider vinegar

1 tablespoon dry mustard

1 teaspoon salt

1/2 teaspoon freshly ground pepper

1/2 teaspoon cayenne pepper or chile caribe (optional)

Combine all the ingredients in a large saucepan and bring to a boil over medium-high heat. Lower the heat and simmer for 1 hour, stirring occasionally. Pour the cooked mixture into a blender and process on low speed until the salsa has a velvety texture. Do not overprocess or the salsa will liquefy! It can be stored in the refrigerator up to 1 week.

Makes 2 to 2 1/4 cups

MESQUITE-GRILLED CORN SALSA

The taste of the Southwest comes through in this fragrant, smoky salsa that is a natural mate for steaks, chicken, or ham barbecued outdoors. Use only authentic mesquite charcoal, placing the corn cobs on the rack when the coals are mostly gray. You can be making this delicious salsa while the meat is cooking.

2 large ears of corn, shucked, with silks removed

Corn oil for brushing

1 ancho chile

1 New Mexico mild green chile

1/2 red bell pepper, seeded and cut into 1/4-inch cubes

1 tablespoon corn oil

1/4 teaspoon cayenne pepper (for hot salsa) or chili powder (for milder salsa)

Brush the corn lightly with oil. Place the corn and chiles on the rack over hot coals and let cook for 6 minutes or until lightly brown in places. Turn frequently. Remove the corn and chiles from the heat. While the ears of corn are cooling, remove the skins from the chiles. Remove the seeds, if desired, and cut the chiles into 1/4-inch cubes. Cut the kernels from the ears of corn; discard the cobs. Combine the corn, chiles, and red bell pepper in a medium bowl. Mix the oil and cayenne or chili powder together in a small bowl and pour it over the salsa. Toss to combine well and serve immediately at room temperature. This salsa can be served hot but should not be served cold because warming brings out the smoky flavor. It can be stored in the refrigerator up to 1 week.

Makes about 1 1/2 cups

NIFTY NECTARINE SALSA

Nectarines seem to be the unsung heroes of the summer fruit brigade. Peaches are more sensuous, their fuzzy surface a delight to the cheek; plums are juicier, seeming to burst at the first bite and requiring much licking of fingers. But the slick, smooth surface of nectarines need not be peeled prior to salsa making, and when truly ripe, their delicate aroma becomes almost perfumelike. Use this salsa to top off hot pork roast sandwiches, to add polish to a mixed-melon fruit salad, or to lend pan-seared catfish some sophistication.

2 nectarines, split, pitted, and cut into 1/4-inch cubes

1/2 cup finely diced pineapple

1 jalapeño chile, seeded and minced

2 teaspoons brown sugar

1 teaspoon rice wine vinegar

1/2 teaspoon grated orange zest

1/2 teaspoon freshly ground pepper

1 teaspoon fresh lemon juice

Combine the nectarines, pineapple, and jalapeño in a medium skillet. In a small bowl mix the remaining ingredients together well except for the lemon juice. Pour the liquid into the skillet, tossing gently to combine. Cook the salsa over medium-low heat for 15 minutes, stirring frequently. Remove from the heat and let cool. Stir in the lemon juice and serve immediately.

Makes about 1 1/2 cups

POTATO-APPLE SALSA

Oh no, not a potato! Yes. This chunky cooked salsa is a savory side dish for pork roast or baked poultry, especially Cornish game hens. I've also served it alongside scrambled eggs and sausage for a hearty winter breakfast. Sure, you can serve rice and beans instead, but isn't this more fun?

3 small red potatoes, peeled and cut into 1/4-inch cubes

3 tablespoons unsalted butter

1/4 cup finely diced red onion

1 New Mexican green chile, roasted, skinned, seeded, and finely diced

1 large tart green apple, peeled, cored, and cut into 1/4-inch cubes

2 tablespoons raisins

1 teaspoon honey

1/2 teaspoon salt

1/4 teaspoon white pepper

1/4 teaspoon cinnamon

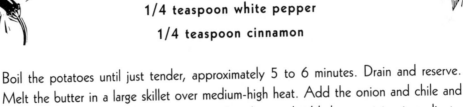

Boil the potatoes until just tender, approximately 5 to 6 minutes. Drain and reserve. Melt the butter in a large skillet over medium-high heat. Add the onion and chile and fry for 2 minutes. Lower the heat to medium-low and add the remaining ingredients. Continue cooking for 2 minutes, stirring frequently. Remove from the heat and let cool. Pour into a serving bowl and use immediately, or cover and refrigerate up to 24 hours.

Makes about 2 cups

RACY RED SALSA

Dried red chiles are normally used to make the complexly seasoned Southwestern sauces for which places like Santa Fe, Albuquerque, and Taos, New Mexico, are justly famous. An enterprising cook once wrote to me inquiring if these sauces could be adapted to a chunkier salsa format. It took quite a bit of experimentation before this recipe was realized. I recommend it for fajitas because they benefit the most from the sauce-salsa balance.

2 dozen dried New Mexico red chiles, stemmed and seeded

2 quarts water

4 cloves garlic, chopped

2 teaspoons chili powder

1/4 cup seeded and finely diced red pepper

1/4 cup finely diced yellow onion

2 green onions (scallions), finely diced

2 tablespoons minced parsley

Place the chiles in a large, deep, ungreased skillet and dry-roast for 2 minutes over medium heat, shaking the pan frequently so the chiles do not blacken. Add the water, lower the heat, and simmer for 15 minutes. Remove the pan from the heat and let the chiles soak for 10 minutes, then strain, discarding the water. Place the chiles in a blender, add the garlic and chili powder, and puree. Strain the mixture over a small bowl, reserving the pulp and discarding the solids. Stir in the remaining ingredients. Return to the pan and warm over low heat for 2 minutes, stirring frequently. Serve immediately.

Makes about 2 cups

RICH RANCHERA SALSA

Spanish hacienda "ranch sauce" is usually ladled inside omelettes or spooned over scrambled eggs. I enjoy it as a dipping sauce for artichoke hearts and deep-fried zucchini.

4 medium tomatoes, each seeded and cut into 8 thick slices
Olive oil for brushing
2 jalapeño chiles, roasted, skinned, and seeded
1/4 cup finely diced yellow onion
1 teaspoon freshly ground pepper
1 teaspoon chili powder
1 teaspoon garlic salt
1 tablespoon olive oil

Preheat the broiler. Lightly brush each side of the tomato slices with olive oil and arrange on a nonstick baking sheet. Broil approximately 4 inches away from the heating element for 2 minutes or just until the slices begin to smoke and lightly brown in spots. Remove from the broiler and let cool to room temperature. Place the tomatoes in a blender with the remaining ingredients except the olive oil and process until thick and pulpy. Heat the oil in a small saucepan, pour in the salsa, and cook for 8 to 9 minutes over medium heat, stirring frequently to avoid sticking, until the liquid is reduced and a thick pulpy salsa forms. Serve immediately. This salsa can be reheated once and should be served warm, not cold or at room temperature, for best flavor. It can be stored in the refrigerator up to 1 week.

Makes about 1 cup

SOUR CREAM SALSA VERDE

One of my favorite guilty pleasures, this luxuriantly rich and creamy salsa has a lovely little tang that complements chicken or cheese enchiladas, steamed vegetables, or a plain pasta side dish. Use only whole milk for an extravagant texture.

6 tomatillos, husked, washed well, and quartered

2 medium green tomatoes, seeded and chopped

2 jalapeño chiles, roasted, half skinned, seeded, and diced

1 serrano chile, seeded and diced

1 New Mexico mild green chile, roasted, skinned, seeded, and diced

1 clove garlic, chopped

1/3 cup whole milk

1/4 cup cilantro

1 teaspoon garlic salt

2 tablespoons canola oil

3 to 4 tablespoons sour cream

Place all the ingredients except the oil and sour cream in a blender and process on medium speed until smooth. Warm the oil in a medium saucepan over medium-high heat. Pour the contents of the blender into the saucepan and cook for about 5 minutes or until thickened. Remove from the heat and immediately stir in the sour cream, mixing well until there are no lumps. Serve immediately.

Makes about 2 cups

SALSA CON QUESO

This dish is perfect for a party table and can be easily doubled. The combination of savory bacon-flavored salsa and hot, gooey cheese is an indulgent delight that will have guests dipping their chips like crazy! The simple original recipe came from a college reunion I attended; this version is sweeter, spicier, and much, much hotter.

1 14-ounce can peeled tomatoes, with juice reserved

4 slices uncooked bacon, chopped into 1/2-inch pieces

1 small yellow onion, finely diced

1 clove garlic, minced

2 Anaheim chiles, roasted, skinned, and cut into 1/4-inch cubes

1 Guero chile, seeded and minced

1 tablespoon oregano

1 tablespoon minced cilantro

1 teaspoon sugar

1/2 teaspoon garlic salt

1/2 teaspoon cayenne pepper

1/2 cup shredded hot pepper Monterey jack cheese

1/2 cup shredded sharp cheddar cheese

Red bell pepper strips for garnish (optional)

Sliced black olives for garnish (optional)

Preheat the oven to 350°F. Chop the tomatoes into 1/4- to 1/2-inch pieces. Fry the bacon in a large skillet over medium-high heat until almost brown, about 4 to 5 minutes. Add the onion and minced garlic and continue cooking, stirring frequently, until the onion turns golden, about 4 minutes. Lower the heat to medium-low and add the remaining ingredients except for the cheeses and garnish, stirring to mix well. Let simmer for 15 minutes, stirring occasionally. Remove from the heat. Pour the skillet contents into a small shallow casserole dish and smother with the cheeses. Place in the oven and cook until the cheeses melt, 6 to 8 minutes. Remove from the oven, decorate with garnish if desired, and serve immediately.

Makes about 2 1/2 cups

COMBINATION SALSAS

BASIC TABLE SALSA

So versatile, this salsa can be served at every meal. Try spooning it onto hot buttered tortillas or crumpets, sprinkling it over eggs or pasta, stirring it into soup. Of course, it goes well with meat, poultry, and fish, too.

4 medium tomatoes, cut into 1/2-inch-thick slices
1 jalapeño chile, roasted and diced
1/2 small white onion, chopped
1 1/2 teaspoons white wine vinegar
1 teaspoon garlic salt

Heat the broiler. Arrange the tomato slices on an ungreased shallow baking pan. Broil the tomatoes approximately 4 inches away from the heating element for 2 minutes or until they turn brown in spots on the top. Remove from the oven and place the tomatoes in a blender. Add the remaining ingredients and process at high speed for 1 minute or until a thick, smooth salsa is formed. Serve immediately or cover and refrigerate up to 1 week. The salsa should be allowed to warm to room temperature before serving.

Makes about 2 cups

Note: Try adding one or more of the following before blending:

1 teaspoon oregano	2 tablespoons chopped parlsey
1 serrano chile	2 cloves garlic
2 tablespoons chopped cilantro	1 tablespoon fresh lime juice
2 sprigs epazote	

BERRY GOOD AVOCADO SALSA

This summertime treat features two of my seasonal favorites: fresh raspberries and creamy Haas avocados. Do not attempt to make this salsa with the smooth-skinned and soapy-tasting Fuerte avocado; the flavor marriage will end in divorce. This elegant salsa is suitable for spooning over duck, goose, pheasant, or roast lamb.

2 tablespoons safflower oil

1 shallot, minced

3 tablespoons raspberry vinegar

1 tablespoon poppy seeds

1 teaspoon sugar

1 large Haas avocado (or 2 small), peeled, pitted, and cut into 1/2-inch cubes

1 pint fresh raspberries, halved if the berries are large

1 poblano chile, roasted, skinned, seeded, and minced

Heat the oil in a small saucepan over medium-high heat. Add the shallots and sauté for 1 minute, stirring frequently. Lower the heat to medium and add the vinegar, poppy seeds, and sugar. Continue cooking for 2 minutes, stirring constantly. Remove from the heat and let cool. Combine the avocado, raspberries, and chile in a medium bowl. Add the vinegar mixture to the bowl and fold gently to coat. Serve immediately. This salsa will not keep.

Makes about 1 3/4 cups

CANNED TOMATILLO SALSA

I can, I can, I can! Only canned tomatillos are available in some parts of the United States, so I've devised this sweetened salsa that simulates the taste of fresh husked tomatoes. For a tarter salsa add the juice of one lime. Serve this salsa verde with roast tenderloin, blackened snapper, or chilled salmon.

1 1/2 cups canned tomatillos, drained and quartered

2 jalapeño chiles, roasted until dark brown in spots and chopped

1 serrano chile, chopped and seeded

1/2 cup water

1/2 cup cilantro

1/4 cup chopped parsley

2 cloves garlic, chopped

2 tablespoons chopped yellow onion

1 teaspoon sugar

1 teaspoon oregano

Place all the ingredients in a blender and process at low speed until a thick, velvety textured green salsa forms. Be careful not to overprocess because these ingredients may liquefy. Serve immediately or cover and refrigerate. If storing this salsa for more than 2 days, mix in 1 teaspoon of fresh lime or lemon juice.

Makes about 2 cups

CARROT-GARLIC SALSA

While I normally recommend freshly grated carrot for most of my salsas, this particular one requires a more softly textured carrot for palatability. This is a highly seasoned salsa for garlic lovers and should be used sparingly to accent beans or simple grilled meats; it can also be stirred into potato or macaroni salad.

4 medium carrots, peeled and cut into 4 pieces

8 cloves garlic, minced

1 tablespoon pimiento

1 tablespoon minced parsley

1 tablespoon olive oil

1 tablespoon tarragon vinegar (or balsamic if necessary)

1/2 teaspoon garlic salt

1/2 teaspoon dill

1/4 teaspoon cayenne pepper

1/4 teaspoon cumin

Cook the carrots in boiling water for 4 to 5 minutes or until just soft. Drain the carrots and plunge them into ice water for 1 minute. Drain the ice water and let the carrots cool completely. When cool, cut the carrots into 1/4-inch cubes. Combine the carrots with the other ingredients, mixing well. Cover and refrigerate for at least 4 hours. Serve cold or at room temperature. This can be stored in the refrigerator up to 4 days.

Makes about 1 cup

CHERIMOYA-LYCHEE SALSA

This exotic fruit salsa is an extravagant luxury and suitable for topping ice cream, cake, roast turkey, or grilled chicken. Its rich, tropical taste is surprisingly bright; use a serrano chile instead of jalapeño for more sunshine and heat!

1 cherimoya, halved, seeded, peeled, and cut into 1/4-inch cubes

12 lychees, peeled, pitted, and finely diced (if canned, then just diced)

1/2 cup finely diced pineapple

1/4 cup pine nuts

1 jalapeño chile, roasted, skinned, seeded, and minced

1 tablespoon maple syrup

1 tablespoon fresh lemon juice

1/2 teaspoon cayenne pepper

Very gently combine the cherimoya, lychees, pineapple, pine nuts, and chile in a medium bowl. In a small bowl mix the remaining ingredients together well into a thin liquid. Pour the liquid over the fruit mixture, gently tossing once or twice to coat. Serve immediately or cover and refrigerate until ready to use. This salsa should be used within 24 hours.

Makes about 2 cups

CHILE PESTO SALSA

Smoky and piquant, this recipe combines the most "flavorable" aspects of pesto with the versatility of salsa. The result is an unusual dipping sauce for vegetables, although I also enjoy it slathered over crackers with cream cheese or tossed with rotelle pasta and Kalamata olives.

1/2 cup pine nuts
10 poblano chiles, roasted, peeled, and seeded
2 medium tomatoes, seeded and quartered
2 cloves garlic
4 tablespoons olive oil
1/2 cup cilantro
1/2 cup chopped parsley
1 tablespoon fresh lemon juice
1 teaspoon garlic salt

Spread the pine nuts on an ungreased baking sheet and place in a preheated broiler about 3 to 4 inches from the heat. Carefully toast the nuts until lightly brown (about 2 minutes), shaking the baking sheet frequently to prevent scorching. Let the nuts cool to room temperature, then combine with the remaining ingredients in a food processor. Process at low speed until thick and fairly smooth, being careful not to liquefy. The salsa can be stored in the refrigerator up to 1 week.

Makes about 2 cups

CHILLED CORN-TURTLE BEAN SALSA

What the buffalo represented to the nomadic tribes of the Plains, corn was to the planting people of the Eastern and Southwestern tribes—an all-nourishing sacred food. Originally derived from a wild grass called *teosintl*, corn was planted in Mexico's Tehuacán Valley as early as eight thousand years ago. While some gringos may have heard some of the hundreds of tales regarding corn personages—such as the Hopi "Corn Mother"—few are acquainted with the term "turtle beans." In modern parlance they are called black beans and have recently become the darling of dining society. I like them because they require no soaking and cook up neat and pretty in about an hour. Unlike refried pintos, these beans should be done al dente so they remain whole, with a faint nutlike flavor. Serve this salsa alongside marinated strip steak or layer it on top of chicken tacos.

3 cups turtle or black beans

1 large yellow onion, roughly chopped

12 cloves garlic, roughly chopped

1 habanero chile, stemmed, seeded, and finely diced

1 cup canned crushed tomatoes with their juice

10 cups water

4 cobs of corn, husked

1/2 red bell pepper, stemmed, seeded, and finely diced

Combine the beans, onion, garlic, chile, and tomatoes in a large pot. Cover with the water and bring to a boil. Lower the heat and continue cooking at a gentle boil for 1 hour or until the beans are just tender to the tooth. Remove from the heat. Drain the liquid and discard; let the remaining bean mixture cool. Remove the kernels from the corncobs by slicing carefully with a paring knife; discard the cobs. Gently mix the beans, corn, and bell pepper together in a large bowl. Cover the bowl with plastic wrap and refrigerate for 2 hours or overnight. This salsa can be stored in the refrigerator up to 4 days.

Makes about 4 cups

FIRE SALSA

Cayenne chiles are red hot, but use the peppers when they're bright green to make this fierce condiment that adds heat to Italian dishes with red sauce, sizzles french fries, and spices rice. Wimps can remove the seeds from the chiles for a milder sauce.

12 cayenne chiles, roasted and skinned
2 medium tomatoes, seeded and quartered
1 clove garlic, chopped
Juice of 1 lemon
2 tablespoons apple cider vinegar

Place all the ingredients in a blender and process until smooth. Serve immediately or cover and refrigerate up to 3 days.

Makes about 1 cup

DRUNKEN SALSA

The wagon; that's what you'll fall off when you make this heady concoction! The chunky salsa is perfect for parties when served with warm tortilla chips or ladled onto nachos. At lunchtime it can even be stirred into tomato soup. Just assign a designated driver!

6 fresh New Mexican long red chiles, roasted, peeled, seeded,
cut into 1/4-inch pieces

6 fresh New Mexican long green chiles, roasted, peeled, seeded,
cut into 1/4-inch pieces

4 green onions (scallions), diced

2 large tomatoes, seeded and cut into 1/2-inch cubes

1/2 small yellow onion, finely chopped

1 clove garlic, minced

1 1/2 ounces tequila

1 tablespoon fresh lime juice

1/2 teaspoon freshly ground pepper

1/2 teaspoon chili powder

Mix all the ingredients well in a medium bowl and serve immediately. It can be stored for only 1 day in the refrigerator.

Makes about 3 cups

EAST INDIAN PIQUANT SALSA

A sophisticated blend of exotic ingredients sure to tempt even the most jaded palates. Ladle it over boiled potatoes, make it a last-minute addition to stir-fry (beef and snow peas are a lovely matchup), or serve it alongside an authentic curry meal.

2 tablespoons unsalted butter

1 medium yellow onion, diced

1/2 teaspoon turmeric

1 teaspoon brown sugar

1/4 cup sherry vinegar (or white wine vinegar with 1 teaspoon sugar)

1/4 cup finely diced pitted dates

1 serrano chile, minced and seeded

10 mandarin orange segments, quartered

Melt the butter in a small skillet over medium-high heat. When it foams, add the onion and cook for 2 minutes, stirring occasionally. Sprinkle the onions with turmeric and sugar. Raise heat to high and continue cooking the onion for 2 more minutes, stirring frequently. Add the vinegar and allow it to boil, stirring frequently until the vinegar volume reduces by half. Lower the heat to medium and add the dates and chile. Cook for 1 minute, stirring constantly. Remove from the heat and let cool. Pour into a small bowl and fold in the orange pieces. Cover and refrigerate for at least 1 hour. It can be stored in the refrigerator for only 1 day.

Makes about 1 cup

GRILLED EGGPLANT SALSA

This excellent salsa can be served as a side dish with barbecued lamb kabobs, atop rice pilaf, or ladled into an omelette with equal aplomb. Grilling and roasting key ingredients give this salsa a unique "outdoorsy" taste. Eggplant can be grilled on a barbecue, of course, but this indoor recipe captures the flavor without the fuss.

1 small eggplant, sliced 1/4 inch thick

Salt

1 cup corn kernels, rinsed well if canned

Olive oil for brushing

3 plum tomatoes, seeded and cut into 1/4-inch cubes

1 poblano chile, roasted just brown in places and minced

2 green onions (scallions), finely diced

2 tablespoons olive oil

2 teaspoons fresh lemon juice

1 teaspoon minced fresh basil leaves or 1/2 teaspoon dried

1 teaspoon minced fresh oregano

Put the eggplant in a colander (over a plate or in the sink) and sprinkle with salt. Let drain for 30 minutes, rinse, and pat dry with paper towels. Preheat the oven to 400°F. Roast the corn kernels in a single layer in a shallow baking pan for 2 minutes, shaking the pan every 30 seconds, until a few kernels have turned golden brown in spots. Remove from the oven and let cool. Turn the oven setting to broil. Brush both sides of the eggplant slices lightly with olive oil. Arrange the slices on a grill rack approximately 6 inches away from

the heating element and broil for 2 to 3 minutes on each side. Remove from the heat and let cool. Cut the eggplant into 1/4-inch cubes and toss with the other ingredients in a medium bowl. Serve warm or at room temperature, or cover and refrigerate up to 2 days.

Makes about 3 cups

IT'S THE GREAT PUMPKIN SEED SALSA

Serve this mildly-spicy salsa over plain pasta or udon noodles, or as a stir-fry side dish.

1 cup raw pumpkin seeds

2 plum tomatoes, cut into 1/4-inch cubes

2 Hungarian wax chiles, roasted, skinned, seeded, and cut into 1/4-inch pieces

2 green onions (scallions), finely diced

1 tablespoon minced cilantro

1 tablespoon peanut oil

2 teaspoons fresh lime juice

Preheat the broiler. Spread the pumpkin seeds on an ungreased shallow baking pan. Place in the oven and broil the seeds until toasted, about 5 minutes, shaking the pan every 30 seconds so that the seeds do not stick. Remove from the oven and let cool. Combine the seeds with the remaining ingredients in a small bowl, mixing well. Serve immediately. The seeds will become rather limp and bland if this salsa is stored for more than 24 hours.

Makes about 1 3/4 cups

HOWLIN' CHAYOTE COYOTE SALSA

A scorchin' serrano chile sets fire to this salsa of contrasting colors and subtle seasoning. This is a good chunky dip, perfect for celery or crackers as well as thicker tortilla chips. If purple bell pepper is not available, red will do. This recipe can be traced back to the (in)famous south-of-the-border chef who created heartburn. Just kidding! He really created afterburn!

1 tablespoon pine nuts

1 chayote, seeded and grated

1/2 small purple bell pepper, seeded and cut into 1/4-inch cubes

1 serrano chile, seeded and minced

1 tablespoon walnut oil

1 teaspoon rice wine vinegar

1 teaspoon lime juice

1 teaspoon minced cilantro

1/4 teaspoon dried savory

1/4 teaspoon dried tarragon

Preheat the oven to 400°F. Spread the pine nuts in an ungreased shallow baking pan and toast in the oven approximately 2 minutes, until golden brown, shaking the pan every 30 seconds so the nuts will not stick. Remove from the oven and let cool. Combine the pine nuts with the chayote and bell pepper in a medium bowl. Combine the remaining ingredients well in a small bowl, then pour over the chayote mixture. Toss to coat and serve immediately or cover and refrigerate, for up to 48 hours only.

Makes about 1 cup

INCA GRAIN SALSA

Quinoa (KEEN-wa) was a staple food of the ancient Incas; its nutlike taste and light consistency has been recently rediscovered by health food fans. Packed with essential amino acids, quinoa is also a complete protein that both vegetarians and meat-eaters can appreciate. It can be found in the rice or gourmet section of most supermarkets. I have used it as a burrito stuffing, to make "rice" pudding, in soup, and to thicken fruit pies with equal success. Used in the salsa below, it stays moist for hours, even outdoors! Serve it with celery sticks or spoon it onto cheese crisps for a hearty appetizer.

1 cup cooked quinoa

1 large tomato, seeded and diced

1/2 cup chopped cilantro

1/2 cup chopped watercress

1/2 cup diced green onions (scallions)

1/4 cup sliced black olives

1/4 cup fresh lemon juice

1/4 cup canola oil

1 teaspoon minced garlic

1/2 teaspoon freshly ground pepper

Mix all the ingredients in a large bowl until thoroughly combined. Cover and refrigerate for 3 hours or overnight. It can be stored up to 3 days in the refrigerator.

Makes about 2 1/2 cups

LARRY'S LENTIL SALSA

A yogi friend of mine loves lentils, so I created this earthy salsa as a surprise for him. While it's lovely ladled over brown rice and vegetables, it can also accompany any meat or poultry as a hearty condiment. For those who think salsa without tomatoes is unthinkable, stir in one finely diced plum tomato with the other ingredients prior to adding the lentils.

1 quart water

1 teaspoon garlic salt

1 cup lentils

1/4 cup finely diced yellow onion

1/4 cup finely diced black olives

1 serrano chile, seeded and minced

1 tablespoon peanut oil

1/2 tablespoon red wine vinegar

1/2 teaspoon chile caribe powder or cayenne pepper

Bring the water and garlic salt to a boil in a medium, deep pot. Add the lentils and turn the heat to low. Cover and simmer for 20 to 25 minutes or until the lentils are just tender. Do not overcook, or the lentils will get mushy. Remove the lentils from the heat, drain, and let cool to room temperature. Combine the remaining ingredients in a medium-size bowl. Gently fold in the lentils and serve, or cover and refrigerate up to 2 days.

Makes about 2 cups

OLLIE, OLLIE, ONION SALSA

Ollie never recaptured his freed oxen, probably because he was too busy spreading this savory salsa on thick slabs of freshly baked bread! Of course, it can accompany virtually any roasted meat or poultry dish, too. I like to spoon it on top of turkey burgers and tuna fish casserole; it can also be combined with bread crumbs and used to stuff game birds.

1 medium red onion, finely diced

4 green onions (scallions), finely diced

1 shallot, finely diced

2 poblano chiles, roasted, skinned, seeded, and minced

2 tablespoons rice wine vinegar

1 tablespoon walnut or sesame oil

1 teaspoon orange honey

1/2 teaspoon cayenne pepper

1/2 teaspoon orange zest

Toss all the ingredients together in a medium bowl and serve immediately. This salsa can be covered and refrigerated up to 4 days before use but should be allowed to warm to room temperature before serving.

Makes 1 to 1 1/4 cups

PASSIONATE PARSLEY SALSA

The humble parsley is often taken for granted, left to languish as a limp garnish as diners dig into more enticing entree items. But its bright flavor and cheery verdant color can be transformed into a succulent sauce, as witnessed here. Use this smooth salsa to complement fish or egg dishes. Some of my guests have slathered it on hot buttered tortillas, too.

3 cups chopped parsley, stems discarded

1 quart water

1 serrano chile, roasted, skinned, seeded, and diced

1 Anaheim chile, roasted, skinned, seeded, and diced

1/4 cup red wine vinegar

1/4 cup canola oil

Juice of 1 lime

Place the parsley and water in a medium saucepan and cook over medium-low heat until wilted. Drain the parsley, place it in a blender, and then add the remaining ingredients. Process on high speed until smooth. It can be stored in the refrigerator up to 3 days.

Makes about 1 cup

PICANTE GREEN CHERRY SALSA

Unripe cherry tomatoes add a zesty tang to this spicy salsa; stir it into rice, layer it into lasagna, or heap it onto hot dogs. It also goes well with nachos. Macho and nacho are two similar Spanish words that should not be confused. When a man is macho, he's supermasculine; when he's nacho, he's covered with melted cheese and chiles.

1 quart green cherry tomatoes, cut into eighths and seeded if necessary
1/4 red bell pepper, seeded and cut into 1/4-inch pieces
1 New Mexican green chile, roasted, skinned, and cut into 1/4-inch pieces
1 red ripe jalapeño chile, seeded, and cut into 1/4-inch pieces
1/4 cup finely diced white onion
2 tablespoons apple cider vinegar
1 tablespoon clover honey
1/2 teaspoon celery seed
1/2 teaspoon allspice
1/2 teaspoon mustard seeds
1/2 teaspoon cinnamon (optional)

Combine the tomatoes, bell pepper, chiles, and onion in a medium bowl. Mix the remaining ingredients together in a small bowl. Pour the liquid over the salsa and stir to coat. Serve immediately or cover and refrigerate overnight. This salsa is best served at room temperature. It can be stored up to 3 days in the refrigerator.

Makes about 2 1/2 cups

PICANTE SALSA

This spicy creation is too chunky to be classified as a hot sauce but carries its inflammable impact into the realm of salsa. Spoon it liberally over chicken breast sandwiches, work it into stir-fried vegetables, or mix it into meatball fixings.

2 pasilla chiles, roasted, skinned, seeded, and chopped

2 New Mexican red chiles (fresh, not dry pod), roasted, skinned, seeded, and chopped

1/2 cup cold water

1 teaspoon fresh lime juice

1/2 teaspoon garlic salt

1/2 teaspoon freshly ground pepper

1/2 teaspoon chili powder

2 cloves garlic, minced

1/2 yellow onion, finely diced

Place all the ingredients except the garlic and onion in a blender and process on low speed until thick and pulpy. If the salsa is too pasty or stiff, add water a teaspoonful at a time until the desired consistency is reached. Pour into a small bowl and stir in the garlic and onion. Use immediately or cover and store in the refrigerator up to 1 week.

Makes about 1 cup

PICANTE SALSA VERDE

Pucker up and savor this sensational hot sauce. This pungent creation is perfect for topping lobster fajitas, ground turkey chimichangas (fried burritos), or poured over prime rib as a heady alternative to horseradish sauce.

1 cup red wine vinegar

1 large red onion, finely diced

6 tomatillos, husked, washed well, and finely diced

1 New Mexico green chile pepper, roasted, skinned, and finely diced

1 clove garlic, minced

1 tablespoon chopped parsley

1 tablespoon chopped cilantro

1 teaspoon ground turmeric

1 teaspoon oregano

1/2 teaspoon cumin

1/2 teaspoon salt

Bring the vinegar to a boil in a medium saucepan. Add the onion and cook for 1 minute. Remove from the heat, add the tomatillos, and let marinate for 1 hour. Pour the salsa into a blender, add the remaining ingredients, and process on low speed until thick and pulpy. Do not overprocess or it will liquefy. Serve immediately or cover and refrigerate up to 1 week. Salsa is best when served at room temperature.

Makes about 1 3/4 cups

PLUM YUMMY SALSA

A neighbor of mine is graced with a very fruitful plum tree and every year I have to think of a new recipe in which to make use of this bountiful harvest. This is the best one yet! It goes gloriously with roast pork, ham steaks, and meatloaf.

1 shallot, minced

2 tablespoons unsalted butter

4 purple plums plus 2 purple plums, peeled, pitted, and cut into 1/4-inch cubes

4 tablespoons brown sugar

1 tablespoon maple syrup

1/4 cup port wine

2 teaspoons rice wine vinegar

1/4 cup golden raisins

2 Italian prune plums, peeled, pitted, and cut into 1/4-inch cubes

1/4 cup red or Bermuda onion, finely diced

1 jalapeño chile, minced and seeded

Fry the shallot in butter in a medium skillet over medium heat for 3 minutes or until soft. Add the 4 purple plums, brown sugar, maple syrup, port wine, vinegar, and raisins. Raise the heat to medium-high and cook for 10 minutes, stirring frequently, or until the sauce thickens. Remove from the heat and let cool. Combine with the remaining ingredients and serve immediately, or refrigerate, covered, for 3 to 5 days.

Makes about 2 cups

ROASTED YELLOW PEPPER SALSA

Roasting lends this salsa a warm, earthy undertone that is brightened by some unexpected spices. Spicy but not unbearably hot, this mixture is an elegant accent to prime rib, venison, and other wild game. So delicious you can even taste it!

1 yellow bell pepper, roasted, skinned, seeded, cut into 1/2-inch pieces

2 jalapeño chiles, roasted, skinned, seeded, cut into 1/4-inch pieces

1 large tomato, seeded and cut into 1/2-inch cubes

1/4 cup chopped cilantro

1 tablespoon olive oil

1 tablespoon fresh lemon juice

1 tablespoon minced fresh dill

1 teaspoon ground fennel

1/2 teaspoon ground cumin

Combine the bell pepper, chiles, tomato, and cilantro in a medium bowl. Mix the remaining ingredients together in a small bowl. Pour over the vegetables and toss gently to coat. Serve immediately, or cover and refrigerate up to 2 days. This salsa should be served at room temperature or warmer.

Makes about 1 3/4 cups

ROASTED CORN AND GARLIC SALSA

This California combo salsa boasts ingredients favored by the Beverly Hills beach set—sun-dried tomatoes and wild mushrooms—but gets its smoky, rich flavor from roasted garlic and corn kernels. Any wild mushroom variety will work, including morel, shiitake, woodear, black cap, and oyster; avoid enoki because they are too tender for salsa treatment. Layer this salsa inside a savory crepe, serve it alongside roast venison, or use it to spiff up spit-roasted beef or lamb. Try using scissors to mince sun-dried tomatoes instead of a knife; they give more control and precision.

4 ears of corn, husked, with silks removed

1 teaspoon corn oil plus more for brushing

1/2 cup diced wild mushrooms (1/4-inch cubes)

1/4 cup oil-packed sun-dried tomatoes, cut into 1/4-inch cubes

2 jalapeño chiles, roasted, skinned, seeded cut into 1/4-inch cubes

1 green onion (scallion), finely diced

3 cloves garlic, roasted, peeled, and minced

1 teaspoon fresh lime juice

1 teaspoon tarragon vinegar

1/2 teaspoon marjoram

1/2 teaspoon garlic salt

1/2 teaspoon lemon pepper

Preheat the broiler. Brush the ears of corn with oil. Place on an ungreased shallow baking pan and broil approximately 6 inches away from the heating element for 10 minutes or until the kernels begin to turn golden brown, making sure to turn the ears frequently. Remove from the heat and let cool. Warm 1 teaspoon of oil in a small skillet over medium-high heat and cook the mushrooms for 6 to 8 minutes, stirring frequently. Remove from the heat and let cool. Cut the corn kernels from the ears and discard the cobs. Combine the corn and mushrooms in a medium bowl and add the chiles, onions, and garlic. Mix well. Combine the remaining ingredients in a small bowl and pour over the vegetables. Stir to mix well and serve at room temperature. This salsa can also be heated and served hot; it should not be kept overnight.

Makes 2 to 2 1/4 cups

ROCKY POINT RELISH SALSA

Sweet mango combines with sharp tomatillos and spicy jalapeño chiles for an unusual but delicious salsa that complements mesquite-grilled sea bass, cornmeal-dressed trout, or any type of broiled tuna steak. Rocky Point is a favorite south-of-the-border haunt of Arizonans; lots of sand makes for wonderful A.T.V. fun! Just don't get sand in your salsa!

1 tablespoon sesame oil

1/2 small yellow onion, diced

2 jalapeño chiles, seeded and diced

6 tomatillos, husked, washed well, and quartered

1 medium mango, peeled, pitted, and chopped

2 tablespoons cilantro

1 teaspoon fresh lemon juice

1 teaspoon brown sugar

Heat the oil in a small skillet over medium-high heat. Add the onion and chiles, and cook until the onion is becoming transparent. Remove from the heat, reserve the onion and chiles, and discard the oil. Combine the remaining ingredients in a food processor until pulpy (they will liquefy if overprocessed). Pour the mixture into a medium bowl. Add the onion and chiles, and stir well to combine. Cover the bowl and refrigerate for 3 hours. It can be stored for only 24 hours in the refrigerator.

Makes about 1 1/2 cups

SAN JUAN SALSA

A friend whose parents came to America from San Juan, Puerto Rico begged me to try my hand at a pineapple-chile relish that was a regional favorite. It was made using both cooked and uncooked ingredients, and had a texture similar to chutney. The end result, featured below, captures the flavor of the sun-kissed Caribbean and is an exceptional topping for any chicken or pork dish.

1 cup plus 3/4 cup diced fresh pineapple, drained
2 teaspoons brown sugar
1 teaspoon rice wine vinegar
1 jalapeño chile, seeded and finely diced
1/2 small green bell pepper, seeded and finely diced
1 carrot, finely grated
Juice of 1 lime
2 tablespoons chopped cilantro
1/4 teaspoon chile caribe powder or ground chili powder

Combine the 1 cup of pineapple, sugar, vinegar, chile, and bell pepper in a medium saucepan. Bring to a boil, stirring frequently, then lower the heat and simmer for 30 minutes, stirring occasionally. Let cool to room temperature. Stir in the 3/4 cup of pineapple and the remaining ingredients, mixing well. Pour into a bowl and serve immediately or cover and refrigerate. This salsa should be used within 2 days or the pineapple will lose its bright flavor.

Makes about 2 cups

SCHIZOPHRENIC SALSA

There are many variations of cooked green chile sauce, but I prefer this one that a friend and I whipped together because it has more body than a traditional cooked sauce and an enhanced flavor. Bacon drippings may be a no-no for many health-conscious readers; simply substitute an equal amount of vegetable shortening. Because this split-personality salsa has both cooked and raw ingredients, it earned the above name. Actually, I'm lying. No, I'm not. Yes, you are! I am not! So there!

1 tablespoon bacon drippings

6 New Mexican green chiles, roasted, skinned, cut into 1/2-inch pieces

1 medium yellow onion, diced

3 medium tomatoes, seeded and diced

1 tomato, seeded and cut into 1/2-inch cubes

1 jalapeño chile, seeded and minced

2 green onions (scallions), finely diced

1 tablespoon chopped cilantro

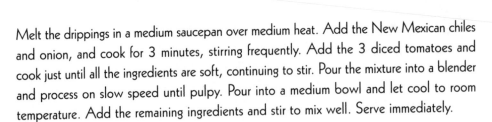

Melt the drippings in a medium saucepan over medium heat. Add the New Mexican chiles and onion, and cook for 3 minutes, stirring frequently. Add the 3 diced tomatoes and cook just until all the ingredients are soft, continuing to stir. Pour the mixture into a blender and process on slow speed until pulpy. Pour into a medium bowl and let cool to room temperature. Add the remaining ingredients and stir to mix well. Serve immediately.

Makes about 2 cups

SPICED TOMATO-RAISIN SALSA

This nice but naughty salsa is perfect for combining with bread crumbs as a poultry stuffing. It can also be enjoyed on its own ladled over roasted chicken or pork roast.

2 tablespoons unsalted butter

1 cup raisins, soaked in warm water for 30 minutes and drained

6 plum tomatoes, seeded and chopped

1/2 cup water

2 teaspoons ground cloves

1 teaspoon cinnamon

1/2 teaspoon salt (optional)

2 tablespoons sherry vinegar or 2 tablespoons white wine
vinegar plus 1 teaspoon of sugar

1 tablespoon brown sugar

1/4 cup finely diced red or Bermuda onion

1 serrano chile, seeded and minced

Melt the butter in a medium saucepan over medium heat. Add the soaked raisins and cook for 2 minutes. Add the tomatoes and continue cooking for 5 minutes, stirring constantly. Lower the heat and add the water, cloves, cinnamon, and salt; simmer for 1 hour, stirring frequently. Remove from the heat. Add the vinegar and brown sugar, stirring until the sugar melts. Stir in the onion and chile. Pour into a bowl and serve warm. It can be stored up to 3 days.

Makes about 2 cups

SUNNY-SIDE UP SALSA

Although originally named for its sunshine-nurtured ingredients, this richly flavorful, Mediterranean-influenced salsa is perfect with egg dishes. I also recommend it highly tossed with cappelini or angel hair pasta, with a bit of feta cheese thrown on top for good measure. Instead of my favorite Kalamata olives, I suggest using more common big greenish black Greek olives because they blend better with the other flavors. To make the olives less salty, soak them in water for six hours, changing the water every thirty minutes. Try using scissors to mince the sun-dried tomatoes instead of a knife; they give more control and precision. Do not add salt to this recipe!

2 tablespoons unsalted sunflower seeds
3/4 cup finely chopped pitted Greek olives
10 oil-packed sun-dried tomatoes, minced
1 serrano chile, seeded and minced
1 teaspoon light olive oil
1/2 teaspoon chopped fresh chives
1/2 teaspoon balsamic vinegar

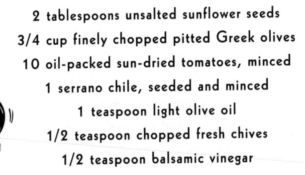

Preheat the oven to 400°F. Spread the sunflower seeds on an ungreased shallow baking pan. Place in the oven and toast until golden, approximately 2 minutes, shaking the pan every 30 seconds so that the seeds don't stick. Remove from the oven and let cool. Combine the seeds and the remaining ingredients in a small bowl, mixing well. Serve immediately. This salsa cannot be stored.

Makes about 1 cup

TAOS GREEN CHILE SALSA

During a visit to the Taos Pueblo in New Mexico, I struck up a conversation with a local masseuse that turned into a dinner invitation. Her enchilada pie was rustic and flavorful, but what I remember most is the fresh-tasting, extremely thick green salsa she prepared from scratch, using chiles grown in her garden. In an attempt to duplicate the recipe, I created this tasty treat that can be layered on hot buttered tortillas, stirred into a bean pot, or folded inside an omelette.

2 large green tomatoes, quartered
2 tomatillos, husked, washed well, and halved
6 New Mexican green chiles, roasted, peeled, and seeded
1 poblano chile, seeded and halved
1 serrano chile, seeded
1/2 teaspoon garlic salt

Place all the ingredients in a blender and process on medium speed until smooth. Add water a teaspoon at a time if the salsa is too thick, or add the juice of 1 lime. Serve immediately or cover and refrigerate until ready to use, up to 1 week.

Makes about 2 cups

TASTE BUD TICKLING TANGERINE SALSA

Tangy, terrific tangerines power this peppery salsa, but its hint of anise makes it memorable. Try it atop stir-fried shrimp and jasmine rice, or serve it alongside barbecued marlin steaks or grilled swordfish. Raspberry vinegar gives this salsa a sweeter flavor.

3 tangerines, peeled, membranes removed, seeded, cut into 1/4-inch cubes
2 Anaheim chiles, roasted, skinned, seeded, and cut into 1/4-inch cubes
1 serrano chile, seeded and minced
1/4 small red onion, finely diced
1 teaspoon sesame oil
1/2 teaspoon tangerine zest
1/2 teaspoon raspberry vinegar
1/2 teaspoon crushed anise seed

Combine all the ingredients in a medium bowl, tossing gently to mix well. Serve immediately or cover and refrigerate. This salsa will usually keep its flavor for 48 hours.

Makes about 1 1/4 cups

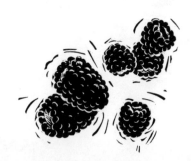

TOMATILLO SALSA

This salsa is the result of refining a recipe given to me by a Zuni housewife who lives about thirty miles south of Gallup, New Mexico. She told me that the Zuni were the first pueblo encountered by the Spanish. When the explorers saw the light adobe walls glistening in the evening sun, they mistakenly thought they'd discovered the fabled seven cities of Cibola, whose streets were paved with gold! This salsa is so versatile, I think it's *worth* its weight in bullion. Use it as a dip for chips or vegetable sticks; spoon it over fettuccine and top with steamed vegetables; smother salmon or halibut steaks.

1 pound tomatillos, husked and washed

1/4 cup cilantro leaves

2 tablespoons chopped parsley

1 tablespoon fresh lemon juice

1 clove garlic, diced

2 serrano chiles, roasted, skinned, seeded, and diced

1/4 teaspoon mustard seeds

1/4 teaspoon fresh ground pepper

Bring 2 quarts of water to a boil in a large pot. Add the tomatillos and simmer until soft, approximately 10 to 15 minutes. Drain the tomatillos, cut in half, and place them with the remaining ingredients in a blender. Blend on high speed until just smooth. Use at room temperature or cover and refrigerate up to 1 week.

Makes about 2 cups

SALSA
COCKTAILS

For those of us who have been caught nipping at the salsa bottle, here's some salsa good enough to drink! Salsa cocktails are a new creation of mine that require a juicer or blender to process. They possess all the spicy heat and flavor punch of uncooked salsa and can be quaffed au naturel or with a shot of gold tequila or pepper vodka added.

While originally intended as an authentically spicy cocktail base for visiting friends, these sassy drinks make a vibrant change from store-bought canned mixed-vegetable juices. Use the ripest, most fragrant ingredients you can find, preferably organically grown or out of your own garden. These drinks can be prepared and stored in clean, sealed glass bottles for up to two days if you do not add alcohol, but they should be savored fresh to obtain maximum nutritional benefits.

All drinks listed below have a tomato juice base; for fresher tasting salsa cocktails, make your own fresh juice. Here's how:

TOMATO JUICE

2 medium red or green tomatoes

Blanche the tomatoes in boiling water for 2 minutes. Peel off the skin and discard. Cut the tomatoes into wedges; remove and discard the seeds. Place the tomato pieces into a blender and process on high speed until liquid, adding a teaspoon of water if necessary; or use a centrifugal juicer, stirring in water after processing.

Makes 1 cup

DEVIL'S DELIGHT SALSA COCKTAIL

2 cups red tomato juice
1 carrot, peeled, blanched, cooled to room temperature, and chopped
1/4 habanero chile, seeded and diced
2 sprigs parsley
1 teaspoon honey
1/2 teaspoon garlic salt
Pineapple wedges for garnish

Place all the ingredients in a blender except pineapple wedges and process at high speed until smooth. If the cocktail is too spicy, add tomato juice 1/2 cup at a time until it reaches acceptable limits; but remember, this drink is for those who like it hot! Fill 2 or more tall glasses with ice and add the salsa cocktail. Garnish the glasses with pineapple wedges and serve.

Makes 2 or more drinks

MEAN GREEN SALSA COCKTAIL

1 cup green tomato juice

1 jalapeño chile, diced and seeded

4 stalks celery, chopped

1/2 clove garlic, chopped

1 tablespoon diced green bell pepper

1 teaspoon fresh lime juice

1/4 teaspoon freshly ground pepper

Cilantro sprigs for garnish

Place all the ingredients in a blender except cilantro sprigs and process on high speed until smooth. Fill 2 tall glasses with ice and fill with the salsa cocktail. Garnish with cilantro sprigs and serve.

Makes 2 drin

PUT UP YOUR CUKES SALSA COCKTAIL

1 cup green tomato juice
1/2 cucumber, peeled, seeded, and chopped
1 green onion (scallion), minced
1 jalapeño chile, seeded and diced
1/8 teaspoon chile caribe powder
Green onion stalks for garnish

Place all the ingredients except green onion stalks in a blender and process on high speed until smooth. Fill 2 tall glasses with ice and add the salsa cocktail. Garnish with a green onion stalk and serve.

Makes 2 drinks

SALSA SMOOTHIE COCKTAIL

1 cup red tomato juice
1/2 avocado, peeled and pitted
2 teaspoons fresh lemon juice
2 teaspoons Worcestershire sauce
1/2 teaspoon cayenne pepper
1/4 teaspoon garlic salt

Place all the ingredients in a blender and process on high speed until smooth. Pour into 2 tall glasses, garnish with a celery stalk, and serve.

Makes 2 drinks

INDEX

ABOUT THE AUTHOR

P. J. Birosik is food editor of the *Sedona Red Rock News*, and credits her salsa savvy to summers spent sampling Tex-Mex cuisine in Ft. Stockston, Texas, during her childhood and teenage years, and numerous vacations in Baja California and mainland Mexico. She is the author of several books including *The Burrito Book*, *Olé Mole*, and *The New Age Music Guide*. She frequently writes on organic gardening, healthy snack foods, and all-natural cooking for numerous publications including, *Whole Life Times* and *Yoga Journal* and is listed in *Who's Who Among Women* and *Who's Who in the West*. P. J. Birosik lives in Sedona, Arizona.